map by palacios

SAN FRANCISCO

HUNTERS POINT

INNES AVE.

3RD ST.

Candlestick Stadium

BAYSHORE FREEWAY

BRISBANE

HEIGHTS

SILVER AVE.

FELTON ST.

JOHN McLAREN PARK

VISITACION AVE.

VISITACION VALLEY

Cow Palace

BAYSHORE

BAYSHORE BLVD.

SAN BRUNO MOUNTAINS

AVALON AVE.

BRAZIL AVE.

NAPLES ST.

GENEVA AVE.

ALEMANY BLVD.

SAN JOSE AVE.

SAN MATEO COUNTY

CANYON

MONTEREY BLVD.

SOUTHERN FREEWAY

City College of S.F.

MT. DAVIDSON

PLYMOUTH AVE.

OCEAN AVE.

CAPITOL AVE.

HOLLOWAY AVE.

MISSION ST.

DALY CITY

GUADALUPE CANYON PARKWAY

EL CAMINO REAL

ST. FRANCIS WOOD

MERCED HEIGHTS

JUNIPERO SERRA BLVD.

JUNIPERO SERRA BLVD.

WAKONA ST.

STERN GROVE

PARK MERCED

BROADMOOR

PINE LAKE

SLOAT BLVD.

LAGUNA DE LA MERCED

LAKE MERCED

SKYLINE FREEWAY

Fleishhacker Pool and Zoo

Fort Funston

SKYLINE BLVD

MUSSEL ROCK

PACIFIC OCEAN

Also by Harold Gilliam

SAN FRANCISCO BAY
SAN FRANCISCO: CITY AT THE GOLDEN GATE
THE FACE OF SAN FRANCISCO

With Photographs by Michael Bry

ISLAND IN TIME: THE POINT REYES PENINSULA
WEATHER OF THE SAN FRANCISCO BAY REGION
THIS CALIFORNIA

The Natural World of
SAN FRANCISCO

The Natural World of

1967

SAN FRANCISCO

Text by HAROLD GILLIAM

Photographs by MICHAEL BRY

DOUBLEDAY & COMPANY, INC., *Garden City, New York*

LIBRARY OF CONGRESS CATALOG CARD NUMBER 66–24328
COPYRIGHT © 1966, 1967 BY HAROLD GILLIAM AND MICHAEL BRY
ALL RIGHTS RESERVED
PRINTED IN THE UNITED STATES OF AMERICA
FIRST EDITION

ACKNOWLEDGMENTS

The writer is deeply grateful to experts in many fields who have generously given of their time and professional knowledge to make this book possible. Foremost among them is the beloved dean of Bay Area naturalists, Mrs. Junea W. Kelly, whose University of California Extension classes "Six Trips Afield" enthralled more than fifteen thousand adult students over a period of forty-four years. A large share of the information in this book was derived from attendance at Mrs. Kelly's classes in the field over several years. Her enthusiasm for nature is matched only by her passion for accuracy, and if this book passes her stern scrutiny without more than a few errors I will count it a success.

For the geological story I am indebted to the U. S. Geologic Survey staff at Menlo Park, particularly Julius Schlocker and Manuel G. Bonilla, whose fascinating geologic maps of the region are available at U.S.G.S. headquarters in San Francisco and elsewhere. Mr. Schlocker's many hours of discussion of the city's geology with the writer were invaluable, although neither he nor the other experts named here are to be held responsible for any inaccuracies I may have committed.

Special thanks are due to the Army Corps of Engineers—notably to Technical Liaison Officer Eugene Huggins; to the University of California Hydraulic Engineering Laboratory; to many members of the staff of the California Academy of Sciences in Golden Gate Park, particularly John Thomas Howell, Curator of Botany and author of the definitive *Flora of San Francisco, California*, the source of much of the plant information in this book; Associate Curator of Botany Elizabeth McClintock, co-author of the popular booklet, *Trees of the Panhandle*; Robert Orr, Associate Director of the Academy and Curator of Ornithology and Mammalogy; and his assistant, Mrs. Hans Schonewald, who made many helpful suggestions for the wildlife chapter.

Members of the San Francisco Recreation and Park Department who have been particularly helpful are Assistant Superintendent of Parks Roy L. Hudson, whose knowledge of Golden Gate Park is unsurpassed and who has given this writer many hours of his time over a period of years; James P. Lang, General Manager; Warren D. Hanson, Public Information Officer; and P. H. "Jock" Brydon, Director of Strybing Arboretum and Botanical Gardens, a plant-lover's paradise, which unfortunately could be mentioned only briefly in these pages but which deserves a book in itself.

Other city officials whose help I want to acknowledge are Brian Fewer, Street Planting and Landscaping Supervisor; James R. McCarthy, Director of City Planning and his staff; and James K. Carr, General Manager of Public Utilities and former U. S. Under Secretary of the Interior.

I am very grateful also to Professor Emeritus Woodbridge Metcalf of the University of California, renowned authority on trees, particularly the eucalyptus; Mrs. Betsy Cutler, ornithologist; C. Robert Elford, State Climatologist; and the late R. Corday Counts, former Meteorologist in Charge at the U. S. Weather Bureau, San Francisco Airport Station.

Mrs. Robert C. DaCosta and other members of the Golden Gate Audubon Society and numerous friends and neighbors, particularly Mrs. Earl F. Bauer, have called my attention to natural features I would otherwise have missed.

My thanks are due also to Michael Bry, whose photographs have sharpened my own perceptions; to Aileen Olsen for typing and editing the manuscript; and to Margot Patterson Doss, author of *San Francisco at Your Feet* and San Francisco *Chronicle* columnist, whose intimate knowledge of the city has been the source of many valuable suggestions.

In addition to the books mentioned above, the following publications will be of special interest to readers; *Birding in the Bay Area,* a booklet by Dale Peters Clyde and Hope Burchard Purmont; *Birds of Golden Gate Park,* by Joseph Mailliard, published by the California Academy of Sciences; *Pacific Discovery,* a magazine also published by the Academy; those excellent regional publications, *Sunset* magazine and Sunset books; and the series of Bay Area Natural History Guides published in paperback by the University of California Press, Arthur C. Smith, editor.

I am grateful to the editors of the San Francisco *Chronicle* for an assignment that has led me into many areas represented in this book and for permission to reprint material that originally appeared in the *Chronicle* Sunday magazine, *This World*. I am also grateful to the San Francisco *Examiner* for permission to use certain of my writings first published in that newspaper.

For invaluable research assistance I want to extend my thanks to the staffs of the *Chronicle* library, the San Francisco Public Library, and the Mechanics Institute Library.

Ann Lawrence Gilliam did a large share of the research for the book and has been my collaborator and guiding star in this as well as in all other projects I have undertaken.

I would like to make the following dedication: to my mother, Vera Gilliam, whose knowledge and enthusiasm for plants and flowers first stimulated my own interest; and to my sons, Gregory and David, to whom I hope I can pass along a similar sense of wonder toward the world of nature.

H. G.

CONTENTS

Acknowledgments   7

Preface   13

Prologue   18

Part One: THE LAND AND THE WATERS   26
    The Franciscan Rocks   26
    The City's Faults   27
    The Blocks Beneath   30
    The Dipping Beds   31
    The Moving Dunes   33
    The River of Sand   34
    The Ocean Margins   35
    The Mystery of the Great Bar   38
    Assault from the Sea   42
    The Green Ridge   45
    Deep Lagoon   47
    The Beach on the Hill   50

Part Two: THE TREES   82
    Tree of Light   82
    The Eucalyptus Rush   84
    Silver Dollars and Shish Kebab   86
    The Raintree   89
    Tree of the Continent's Edge   93
    Yerba Buena   96
    "Woods for Murderers"   97

CONTENTS

Part Three: THE PARKS   118
   The Vision of Frederick Law Olmsted   118
   The Faith of William Hammond Hall   120
   The Park and the Politicians   123
   The McLaren Legend   127
   Uncle John's Rocks   129
   Mike de Young's Gamble   130
   The Return of the Tea Garden   131
   High Wilderness   133
   Birthplace of the City   135
   Rim of the Continent   138

Part Four: THE WILDLIFE   150
   The Nocturnalists   150
   The Passing of the "Seals"   152
   Theme and Variations   154
   Feathered Artists   156
   The Ducks and the Phoenix   158
   Birds of Pleasure   160
   Gull Talk   162
   When the Swallows Come Back . . .   164
   . . . To Lake Merced   166

Part Five: THE SKY   194
   The Great Procession   194
   Low and High, Wet and Dry   196
   Aerial Spectacular   199
   Second Spring   201
   The Winds of the City   203
   The Meeting of the Seasons   206

Epilogue   245

Index   249

1 2

PREFACE

Doubtless a major cause of the spiritual discontent of our times is the fact that urban man spends most of his days in his own hive, sealed off from the sources of physical and spiritual nourishment in the natural world. Many a denizen of these hives never in the course of his daily activities sets foot on the soil or looks up at the branches of a tree or sees a wild animal. He catches not even a glimpse of a rushing stream or a breaking wave or a rising tide, and he has no notion which way the great currents of air are moving over his head.

Despite his best efforts, however, man finds it impossible to cut himself off from nature completely. His bodily rhythms are the rhythms of the turning planet and the changing seasons, the migrating flocks and the flowing waters. For all but the last few generations of his millenniums on earth, man has lived in the wilderness or followed the herds or tilled the soil, and now, in this most recent moment of his existence he cannot with impunity seal himself away from the elements that gave him nurture. The toll of such attempted isolation is high. The diseases of overcivilization are endemic in our cities—hypertension, ulcers, arteriosclerosis, heart trouble, nervous breakdowns, and, over all, an undefinable persistent rootlessness, a sense of alienation from anything permanent and abiding.

The urban mode of living is not entirely to blame for this alienation, however. With some effort the resident of almost any city, by making good use of all his senses, by sharpening his perceptions, can find, here and there, nourishment in such enclaves of nature as have not been obliterated by the asphaltic tide of progress. In this respect San Francisco is more fortunate than most other cities. It is one of the most densely populated areas in the United States—outranked in this respect only by the vertical hives around New York and Chicago—and there are neighborhoods here where you can walk for blocks without seeing a green leaf or a blade of grass. Yet topography has made it almost impossible for the San Franciscan to ignore nature completely. The heights of the city make it well-nigh compulsory for him to look out on the surrounding waters and the distant hills. The air may be clear, offering uninterrupted views of forested mountains fifty miles away, or it may be full of moving vapors, and you can see the currents flowing in regular cycles across the water and over the land.

Stretching halfway across the city itself is the green wonderland of Golden Gate Park, possibly man's greatest visible achievement on this peninsula. Here and there throughout the city, among asphalt and concrete and long blocks of wall-to-wall houses, are small parks frequented by legions of birds; there are open spaces where the wind ripples the sand, small animals burrow, and after the first rains the air is fragrant with sweet alyssum. There are still undeveloped hillsides where through the seasons you can watch the grasses rise and flourish and wither, where you can see richly contorted outcrops of the underlying rock of this peninsula.

And so with sharpened senses and whetted tastes you can regain an awareness of the outer world. You can escape the myopia that results from staring at papers too long, the dulled vision that comes of looking no farther than the wall of the room or the building across the street. You can rediscover a sense of hearing which may have been benumbed by the roar of traffic, a sense of smell blunted by smoke and urban stenches. You can learn again the forgotten rhythms of the natural world. You can attain the perspective that comes of seeing the whole of things, the richness of emotion that arises from a broadening of experience and an extension of sympathies, the vitality that derives from immediate contact with the life force.

Inevitably there are counter life forces in motion; there are people so blinded by the narrow confines of the hive that they are determined, while waving the banners of progress, to obliterate all vestiges of nature from this environment, to fill the last bird marshes, build over the final hillsides, invade the green spaces with buildings and parking lots and freeways. The resulting loss of our natural heritage would condemn future generations to the myopia of the hive, to a life of spiritual malnutrition. This book is

14

dedicated to the proposition that a humane urban environment must offer a proper balance between the works of man and the works of nature, that the best city is the one that does not so thoroughly surround its residents with the transitory, the ephemeral, the ugly—with noise, smoke, clutter, concrete, and asphalt—that they are unable to make contact with the great world outside.

It would seem fitting that some sizable natural area should be set aside as part of the city's park system, dedicated not to horticulture and landscaping but to the preservation of a sample of the indigenous plant and animal life and land forms of the region, an outdoor museum where children and adults could see what this peninsula looked like before the concrete and asphalt were spread to its farthest corners.

This book is not a natural history of the city. Readers familiar with Linnaeus had best look elsewhere for a classification of the species found in this region, for a checklist of birds or an analysis of botanical features. Here we will simply look at a few aspects of nature in San Francisco, describe some places where the web of life is visible, speculate on a few of the most common kinds of trees and animals and land forms, hoping to generate in the reader a curiosity that will provoke him to undertake his own explorations, to make his own discoveries, to develop a keener sense of the natural wonders around him in this or any crowded city—and, we may hope, to join in the defense of nature when it is threatened by the bulldozers.

The Natural World of
SAN FRANCISCO

PROLOGUE

The wet sand is springy under foot and gives a rollicking rhythm to your step as you walk down the wide flat expanse of beach. South of Fleishhacker Zoo the cliffs begin to rise behind the beach, and civilization vanishes. If you had walked here a thousand years ago, the scene would have scarcely been different. You can see only the high, dun-colored escarpment with its twisted strata, the broad acres of flat strand left bare by a minus tide, and the booming surf. Six hours earlier, the surface of the ocean stood higher than you can now reach above your head. The moon is closer than it has been during the past twelve months, and its gravitational attraction sets up the year's greatest range of tides—eight and a half feet between the highest and the lowest.

Now, thin films of water draining off the sand make it a mirror reflecting the pale winter sun and the mists overhead. Looking down, you feel as if you were walking through the sky, using the clouds as stepping stones. At the water's edge is a covey of sea birds, big gray and white gulls, standing nearly motionless, all facing north into the breeze like soldiers in formation, each one reflected as an inverted image in the sand mirror. Among them dart small round turnstones, their short legs moving so rapidly as to be almost invisible. Two hundred yards offshore a giant swell rises and grows into a mountain of water as it crosses the shoaling bottom. Its front becomes increasingly steeper until it seems impossibly top-heavy, but it continues to rise, cuts off the view of the ocean beyond, and itself becomes the horizon.

Then a series of events occurs so rapidly that you are not quite sure of the sequence. A thin line of foam appears along the rim; almost simultaneously, curving banners of spindrift are ripped from the crest by the breeze and billow five and ten feet into the air like voluminous white veils. The crest plunges forward and for an indelible instant of time the declining sun shines through the smooth curving body of the wave, turning it into an opalescent green-gold. The curve is completed at one point and, with a rapid down-looping effect like a scalloped curtain descending unevenly, the break spreads along the entire wave front in both directions.

Thunderous volleys echo along the shore; the entire wave becomes a mass of churning white, racing toward the beach. At its rear, white plumes rise into the air on the rebound. Nearing the shore, it diminishes in size and sound and rolls more slowly across the shallows, finally dying in swirling patterns on the flat sand at your feet. This is the plunging type of breaker that comes from hundreds or even thousands of miles at sea. Doubtless the source was a series of storms that have been moving past the Hawaiian Islands and heading northeast to hit the coasts of Washington and Oregon, avoiding most of California but sending these wave trains ashore as a sign of their passing.

You set off again along the hard resilient sand, sidestepping the scores of brittle white sand dollars that have washed up along this section of the beach—each the "skeleton" of an animal that once dwelt in the beds on the ocean bottom, straining the water for edible plankton. The film of water draining off the sand refines the colors of the grains beneath—browns and tans and rich reds set off by streaks of jet black and blended with the reflected lights of the sky, pale golds and smoky grays and merging tones of pearl and amber.

The receding water also creates shallow contours in the sand. When it strikes a pebble or a shell fragment, the cleft current sets up a V-shaped flow, etching into the sand diverging lines. The lines intersect and overlap with others to form herringbone patterns in intriguing geometrical complications with as many elaborations as a Bach fugue. Then a spent wave sweeps slowly over the surface like a windshield wiper, erasing the markings but creating new patterns as it returns to the sea.

Ahead of you on the sand is a big dead crab left by the ebbing tide. The odd markings on its purple carapace oddly resemble a contorted face,

1 9

and you are reminded of the species of oriental crab that had a figure on its shell vaguely resembling a portrait of an ancient Japanese deity. Superstitious fishermen threw back crabs that chanced to have markings like these until over the centuries a whole race of them evolved and the portrait became perfected.

Farther down the beach you come across another swarm of gulls standing near the water but instead of facing north toward the Golden Gate, these all face the cliffs, where a breeze comes through a shallow pass. The birds' formation is a sign of the drainage of air that flows at this time of year from the cold inner valleys to the warmer sea through the passes in the Coast Range—such as the Golden Gate or, in this case, Alemany Gap.

The sun sinks into the mists over the ocean, and the twilight deepens quickly. Ahead down the beach you can dimly make out the big black shape of Mussel Rock, like a stranded ship just offshore. Here, for some reason you do not immediately discern, the aspect of the shoreline begins to change. The beach becomes narrow and rocky; the breeze turns into a wind; offshore the waves break over outcrops of jagged boulders, sending sheets of spray into the air.

A huge wave roars out of the darkness, and you are unable to outrun it on the cobble-covered beach. The churning water swirls around your ankles and reaches up around your knees like invisible hands to pull you down. Then the wave spends itself, and as you reach the foot of the cliff the reason for the changed aspect of the shore becomes suddenly apparent. Cleaving the escarpment ahead of you is a deep V-shaped canyon opening onto the beach. The wind is howling through it with nearly enough force to knock you down. The farther reaches of the canyon are invisible in the gloom, but you realize now that you are standing precisely on the San Andreas Fault.

Slicing northward up the peninsula, the great earthquake rift comes out to sea here and continues straight across the Gulf of the Farallones to the Marin shore at Bolinas. The offshore rocks here are part of a harder, more resistant formation on the west side of the fault. At Mussel Rock just ahead, the waves have carved caves and gorges and caverns where the roaring surf resonates against unseen surfaces. You clamber over rocks covered with mussels, ribbon kelp, and starfish, and walk through low-ceilinged

2 0

tunnels where the waves pound and swirl at all times except during such an extreme minus tide as this.

Exploring the weird rock formations, you become vaguely conscious of an odor brought on the wind, a scent of decay and death. Now, just inshore alongside the big rocks, you find the source, a landslide whose base is strewn with the rubble of civilization—a garbage dump. Quickly you leave the area and walk back up the beach, wondering at the venality of the human species.

Out over the ocean the bright sphere of Venus gleams frostily through the overcast. On the darkened horizon, far out to sea, there are the pinpoint flashes of the warning lights—the beam from the lightship a dozen miles offshore and the dimmer, more distant signal of the beacon on the Farallones. Slowly a misty full moon comes into sight over the cliff. A few hours from now it will be directly overhead, drawing the waters of the ocean like a magnet in the sky, and the responding tides will once again cover this beach.

It occurs to you as you walk the flat beach under the cliff in the light of the rising moon that the human animal is doubtless venal and vicious but he is also at times capable of splendor. He is the climax, thus far, of the great chain of life you have observed on this beach. Out of the watery chaos of the ocean and the paroxysms of the earth's crust came the succession of evolving species, the sand dollar, the crab, the sea birds, and, finally, man. Finally? Maybe not. It does not seem likely that the immemorial process has come to an end. Maybe it is the role of man, at least contemporary man, to point the way toward some higher form of life, some greater destiny not yet conceivable.

Far offshore, veils of spindrift rise into the moonlight as a colossal wave breaks and charges ashore, sweeping with a rush across the flat expanse of beach. The spheres are swinging along their appointed orbits: the moon is climbing toward the zenith; the tide is rising; the sea is about to reclaim its rightful dominion over the beach; and you hurry along ahead of the advancing waves, skirting the foot of the cliff.

This is a densely populated city, where people live and work in vertical hives, crowded together on the tip of a peninsula.

But it is also a city surrounded by space, where the rhythms of the natural world are visible and audible. Along its western margin, ground swells from far Pacific storms break into long combers with the rolling thunder of a thousand drums.

Beyond the sea wall, waves burst into explosive patterns of visible energy within sight of the downtown skyscrapers, and the changing waters of the bay gleam in the sun or grow dark under a cloud in a perpetual spectacle of shifting lights and textures.

To the south are rolling hills, covered with waving grasses, chaparral and wildflowers.

Beyond the bay, visible from the heights of the city, are ranges of encircling mountains.

There you can wander among slopes and forests of live oak, Douglas fir, and redwood.

Part One

THE LAND AND THE WATERS

The Franciscan Rocks

San Francisco is a city of the sea geologically as well as historically. The tides sweep its sea walls; the rocks beneath it were created, layer by layer, on the bottom of the ocean and literally rose from the sea.

About one hundred million years ago the San Francisco area and the entire present California coast were at the bottom of the Pacific Ocean, more than a mile deep. The edge of the continent was about one hundred miles to the east, on the slopes of the low mountain range that eventually became the Sierra Nevada. As this ancestral Sierra rose under the pressure of forces deep in the earth's crust, heavy rains fell on the range. The runoff carved deep gullies and canyons, and rivers flowed full of gravel, sand, and mud to the sea. There the currents distributed the debris over a broad area of the ocean floor.

Over the millenniums the sediments formed layer after layer and solidified as rock to depths of thousands of feet. Volcanic eruptions on the ocean floor heaved up some of the bedded layers, jumbling various types of rocks together. The floor of the ocean gradually sagged beneath the load, and the sediments from the rising Sierra continued to be deposited on the subsiding sea bottom until in some places they were an incredible ten miles deep.

This colossal shifting of the weight load on the earth's crust eventually caused the sea floor to buckle and break. Some areas were raised above the surface of the ocean, forming islands and peninsulas. This region rose above sea level and fell below it again many times over a period of tens of millions of years before the Coast Range, in which San Francisco is located, began to take its present shape during the Pleistocene epoch, the past million years.

Until recently it was believed that most of the Coast Range sediments had been eroded from an offshore land mass known as Salinia, represented today by the residual granitic rocks of the Farallon Islands, twenty-five miles offshore, and the related rocks of the Point Reyes Peninsula to the north. However, new techniques of dating the granitic rocks show them to be younger than much of the Coast Range formation. This and other evidence causes geologists to believe that the rising Sierra Nevada was the principal source.

Although the rock layers that had been deposited on the bed of that ancient sea extend for hundreds of miles along the California and Oregon coasts, geologists first discovered them in San Francisco and named them the Franciscan formation. These rocks give San Francisco the qualities that make it geographically unique—its hills and valleys, its precipitous streets, its panoramas of land and water. Look closely as you climb Telegraph Hill or Twin Peaks and you can see, in roadcuts and outcrops, the layered or massive rocks that were laid down beneath Cretaceous seas and were ultimately thrust above the ocean to form this new edge of the continent.

The City's Faults

Over the eons, as the Franciscan rocks were lifted, twisted, folded, and contorted, they fractured into blocks, both large and small. The processes that created these contours are still taking place, and when the blocks move suddenly along the larger fractures—or faults—owing to pent-up strains deep in the earth, the result is an earthquake. The 1906 San Francisco earthquake was but one of many recorded movements of major earth blocks along the San Andreas Fault. The San Andreas, named for a valley just south of San Francisco, where it was first identified a dozen years before the 1906 disaster, extends for six hundred miles from Cape Mendocino to the Gulf of California, but it does not appear within San Francisco itself, crossing the ocean floor just off the Golden Gate.

There are lesser faults within the city, however, ranging from thousands of visible cracks that appear in all rock masses to two major rupture zones extending entirely across the peninsula on which the city stands. These two were unknown until rock detectives of the United States Geologic Survey covered the city block by block over a period of several years beginning in 1948. Julius Schlocker and Manuel G. Bonilla, assisted by Mrs. Dorothy Radbruch, had the assignment of identifying every type of rock and soil beneath the city.

Early in the work Schlocker became curious about a peculiarity in the northern part of the city. In a previously known belt of serpentine rock he found large quantities of other rock types that were extremely sheared and mixed in variety, as if they had been sliced and scrambled by some immense subterranean pressures. The belt seemed to be about a mile wide, extending from Hunters Point northwest across the city to Fort Point at the Golden Gate. Later Schlocker discovered a narrow extension of the same zone in the cliffs north of the Golden Gate and another extension southeast of Hunters Point for several miles beneath the waters of San Francisco Bay. He also found that bedrock north of the serpentine belt was entirely different from bedrock to the south.

All these signs seemed to point to one conclusion: the existence of a previously undiscovered earthquake fault. Like most big faults, including the San Andreas (which here runs offshore), this one was not a single crack in the earth, but a broad zone of rocks that had been fractured over the eons by grinding action, presumably during sporadic quakes.

Later Bonilla, exploring in the vicinity of McLaren Park, near the city's southeastern corner, noticed near Persia Avenue an odd-looking roadcut. He noted here some of the same signs Schlocker had found in the serpentine belt: sheared rock, as many varieties as a sack of mixed nuts, and different kinds of bedrock on either side of the shear zone—a difference Bonilla discovered by a series of laboratory tests. To the northwest Bonilla found other intermittent exposures, extending from the edge of the bay near the Cow Palace, up Visitacion Valley (a depression possibly created by erosion along the fault) to San Francisco City College, then across a southwestern spur of Mount Davidson to the vicinity of Lincoln High School in the Sunset district. From there on, any traces of the fault were hidden by the built-over sand dunes of the Sunset. Bonilla named the rift zone the City College Fault.

Looking over Bonilla's work, Schlocker was struck by another coincidence.

A slightly curved extension of the fault zone through the sand dunes would connect with a known fault area at Land's End northeast of the Cliff House, separating the same two kinds of bedrock. It seemed significant that the City College and Hunters Point-Fort Point faults, about three miles apart, were roughly parallel. Were the faults still active? Schlocker felt that the Hunters Point-Fort Point Fault was an ancient rift, no longer active. But Bonilla was less certain about the City College Fault, noting that epicenters of some recent minor earthquakes had been approximately located near the fault line. Whether the fault was active or not, however, he was convinced that engineers and builders along the fault should take extra precautions. Bedrock there may not be as solid as it seems, and landsliding is a danger in steep cuts and excavations.

The two geologists also found that existence of faults in these two locations would help explain another strange phenomenon.

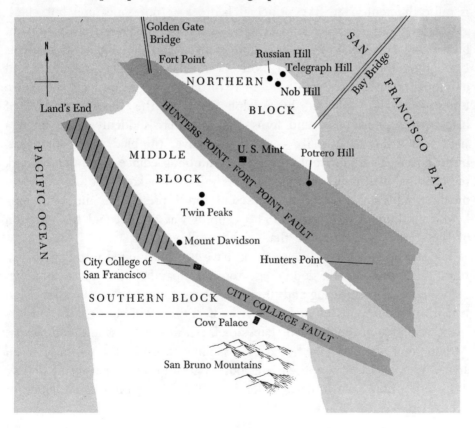

The Blocks Beneath

The two fault zones running diagonally across the peninsula divide the city into three main blocks, composed of different kinds of rock. Anyone with a sharp eye will notice that Telegraph Hill, for example, is composed of quite different rock than that found on Twin Peaks. In the old quarries on the east side of Telegraph Hill you can see massive sandstone strata, sometimes ten feet and more in thickness, separated by thin layers of shale. Each bed of sandstone represents the accumulated deposits of innumerable grains of sand, washed to the ocean floor from the rising Sierra Nevada. The shale resulted from intermittent deposits of fine clay rather than sand.

Bedrock similar to that found on Telegraph Hill is found also in the city's southern block, but the middle block, between the two fault zones, is quite different. Here the principal bedrock is not sandstone but chert, a thin-layered rock that is most often dark red but may have tints of brown and gray or bright yellow and orange. You can see it in roadcuts throughout the block, but the most spectacular occurrence of chert is in outcrops on Mount Sutro. Wander through the near-jungle of Sutro Forest—eucalyptus planted by Adolph Sutro in the 1890s, brambles of blackberries, poison oak, and ferns—and you may suddenly come upon a sight so startling as to make you feel you have stumbled across some prehistoric ruin. There in front of you is a crumbling edifice of laminated dark red chert as intricately sculptured as the walls of Angkor Wat. The carvings on these walls are abstract and represent forces present on the earth long before the human race arrived. The sculptor was nature, and the duration of the work has been more than eighty million years.

The strata, each a few inches thick, have been fashioned into superb textures and forms—arches, domes, chevrons, and parabolas, all given innumerable variations by shearing and slumping, by swellings and compressions, and by intrusions of veins of rock materials of entirely different colors and textures, resulting in rough-hewn shapes of incredible richness and complexity. At one point a wall is penetrated by a shallow cave like the entrance to an arched temple. Elsewhere there are roofless corridors between disintegrating walls and striking contrasts of color in green lichens on red or yellow or ochre rock.

Between the beds of chert, which may be one to five inches thick, are thin layers of shale. Embedded in most of the chert strata, lighter colored than the rock and barely visible, are billions of fossils of some of our earliest ancestors—radiolarians, one-celled animals that dwelt in the ocean when this rock was in the process of formation. You can see the splendidly sculptured radiolarian chert also on Sunset Heights (Golden Gate Heights), the long ridge west of Twin Peaks; on such hills as Mount Olympus, Tank Hill near Seventeenth and Clayton, Corona Heights above the Junior Museum; and in Golden Gate Park on Strawberry Hill above Stow Lake, at the Prayer-book Cross, and at Quarry Lake, where the beds are penetrated in places by some wonderfully contorted roots of Monterey pines.

The chert, like the sandstone, was also formed on the ocean floor, although not by the deposit of sand. It was a by-product of the volcanic activity that took place on the sea bottom. Molten lava, pouring through innumerable rifts in the ocean floor, heated the water. The hot water dissolved part of the lava, which separated out and became chert. The lava itself is still present as volcanic rock and visible in association with the chert. Like the chert it is often reddish brown, but it is softer and is not thinly layered. Owing to the chemical process that took place more than one hundred million years ago on the bottom of that ancient sea, the chert is considerably harder and more resistant to erosion than sandstone and other rocks. As a result the city's highest summits—primarily the ridges topped by Mount Sutro, Twin Peaks, and Mount Davidson—are those in the middle block where chert is the principal bedrock.

The Dipping Beds

There is a particularly odd feature of the city's middle block that geologists are at a loss to explain. Like most strata, those of the chert have been rumpled and pressured by crustal forces into folds ranging from a few inches to miles in extent. In the sandstone blocks on either side, as in most other regions of the Coast Range, the folds of the strata are aligned in the same direction as the axis of the range itself—northwest and southeast. But in this central block the folds are aligned either north and south or east and west, evidently twisted by horizontal slippage along the faults.

31

One good place to see the dip of the beds is on Twin Peaks Boulevard. Climbing the road from the north, you can see in roadcuts and outcrops the smooth top surface of the beds exposed like overlapping inch-thick sheets dipping northward. On the reverse or southern side of the outcrops or ridges, however, only the sharp jagged edges of the broken strata are visible, pointing up to the south. These strata, like those throughout the city, represent rocks that were once overlain by thousands of feet of other beds and have been exposed as the upper strata were eroded away. San Francisco's hills probably were created not by the folding of rocks at the surface but by the carving of gulleys, canyons, and valleys in strata which had been folded long before they rose above the sea.

Stand on Twin Peaks and visualize the original rocks lying far above your head, the rains and winds slowly washing them away. The rocks most resistant to erosion, primarily because they consist of the hard chert, are those that stand today as the hills beneath your feet and nearby summits. The city's lower summits, such as Russian, Nob, and Telegraph hills, are primarily sandstone, more easily eroded than the chert.

Look south, however, and you face an inconsistency. The southern block rises to heights several hundred feet greater than the summit on which you stand. The highest point of the San Bruno Mountains, which lie just south of the city limits, is 1314 feet, compared to 922 feet for Twin Peaks and 938 for Mount Davidson. Yet the San Bruno Mountains and the entire southern block, like Nob Hill and the northern block, consist of sandstone, which is less resistant to erosion than the chert and theoretically should have been worn down by this time to a much lower level.

The explanation probably lies in two faults the geologists have discovered along the San Bruno range, paralleling the ridge on the south. Evidently this sandstone block was thrust upward along these faults during some long-ago period of crustal disturbance, raising the ridge into the sky. It is being eroded away steadily, however, and in time may be worn down to lower elevations than the harder chert summits of the middle block. This assumption presumes there is no further movement along these faults, but it is conceivable the block may rise still higher along the faults and gain additional elevation. In any case, as you stand on these peaks remember that in the long perspectives of geologic time you are merely standing on the crest of a wave that is momentarily higher than the surrounding area. Your geographic eminence will last but a fraction of a second of geologic time; make the most of it.

The Moving Dunes

San Francisco's major summits are in effect islands in a sea of sand. This city is literally founded on sand, and the peaks are isolated outcrops of bedrock protruding above the rolling dunes. The eighteenth-century explorers noted that the area consisted principally of dunes, and the first Forty-Niners often were disgusted to find their tents and shanties half buried in the drifts. The perennial sea wind, roaring across the tip of the peninsula for eons, had brought with it two elements created by the ocean—the flowing fog and the drifting sand. Like the fog, the sand was borne by the wind eastward over the peninsula, encountered obstacles in the form of rocky ridges and outcrops, piled into drifts, swirled into eddies, rose up the seaward side of the higher hills, flowed profusely through gaps and passes, and poured down the leeward slopes in a slow flood.

As the sand moved up from the ocean, filling canyons and leveling valleys, it created the smooth slopes of the Richmond and Sunset districts. The high area in the Richmond now occupied by George Washington High School, for example, is a volcanic outcrop surrounded by drifted sand. Farther south the sand flow encountered the long north-south ridge known as Sunset Heights, or Golden Gate Heights—consisting mainly of chert. So powerful and persistent was the sea wind that it carried the sands up the ridge several hundred feet. At some points the flow rose entirely over the ridge at the extraordinary height of six hundred feet and spilled down the leeward slope toward Laguna Honda canyon, creating drifts that sometimes still give trouble to residents of houses built in that area.

Protected from the flow by this barrier, Mount Sutro and most of Twin Peaks are relatively free of sand. But in the unprotected low-lying valleys to the north now occupied by Golden Gate Park and California Street, the flow was abundant. The moving sand hit a volcanic outcrop at Buena Vista Peak, rose five hundred feet to the peak's top, and spilled down the lee side toward the valley of the Mission district. Most of the Mission, sheltered by the Twin Peaks-Mount Davidson Ridge, escaped the sand flood. Farther

33

north the sand drifted through Hayes Valley to the Civic Center area in tremendous quantities. The City Hall is built on sand eighty feet deep.

In the eastern or leeward part of the city, where the wind is less powerful, the sand flowed around, rather than over, the higher areas of Russian, Nob, and Telegraph hills, but in such low areas as Polk Gulch and the valley now occupied by Market Street, the flow was unobstructed. Near the site of the Palace Hotel, it created a large dune that impeded travel in Gold Rush times, forcing traffic for Mission Dolores to detour to the south. The dune had to be leveled when Market Street was built. Eastward the sand flood continued, washed up on the shores of Rincon Hill (now the Bay Bridge anchorage), and proceeded to the original edge of the Bay itself. Thus the great sand flow borne on the sea winds extended at this point entirely across the peninsula, a distance of about seven miles—the longest drift on the Pacific coast.

The dune sand, of course, was spread over older landscapes of rock and soil which were doubtless far steeper and more varied than the present subdued contours. The blowing sand filled in the valleys, smoothed over the canyons, and drifted around the high points. But the sand itself created rolling contours. Some of the original dunes in the Sunset district were seventy-five feet high, and the total depth of the sand exceeded one hundred feet. In other areas the sand is very shallow. In parts of Golden Gate Park, for example, it is only a few feet in depth; and in some areas, such as Quarry Lake, Prayerbook Cross, and Strawberry Hill, outcrops rise above it. Probably beneath the sand the contours of the land in the western areas are as precipitous as present contours in the eastern part of the city, and there may well be counterparts of Telegraph, Russian, and Nob hills buried beneath the undulating Sahara-like dunes of the Sunset and Richmond districts.

The River of Sand

Any such sand flow, extending over a period of thousands of years, would need an almost illimitable source. Its immediate source was Ocean Beach, the long strand stretching for several miles south of Cliff House. But Ocean Beach itself is continually resupplied. Off the California coast, as off most coasts of the world, there is a perennial "river of sand" carried along the shore by the prevailing currents. In low-lying areas the sand grains are deposited by the waves, creating beaches. But the sand river in turn must have its own source of supply. For thousands of years the giant combers from the far Pacific have battered the edge of the continent with such force as to disintegrate the coastal rocks and cliffs and grind them into sand. The cliffs along the peninsula south of San Francisco steadily retreat as they are converted into sand which is carried north by the currents and deposited on Ocean Beach, where it can be picked up by the wind. The result, in the long epochs of geological time, was to transfer large parts of the peninsula to San Francisco, and the city is largely built on real estate taken from San Mateo County, immediately south.

The sand flow came to an end relatively recently. It was brought to a halt largely by the initiative of two men, William Hammond Hall, founder of Golden Gate Park, and his successor, John McLaren. In their long battles to reclaim Golden Gate Park from the dunes, they found that the drifting sand continually covered their new plantings. They sowed grasses that succeeded in stemming the moving dunes to some degree, but the flow was not stopped until Hall conceived and began construction of a "dam" along the ocean. Workmen planted two lines of timbers in the dunes just back of the beach and connected them with wire mesh. Into the spaces between, they dumped cuttings, rock, and other debris from the park. The drifting sand filled the spaces until a long dike was created, too steep for the sand to surmount. In later years the present concrete sea wall was built, and the Great Highway was completed in 1929 along the top of the dike. Cut off from their source by the barrier, the dunes in the western part of the city ceased to grow, and nearly all of them have been built over.

The Ocean Margins

The narrow strips of sand along the margins of the great oceans are the most changeable regions of the earth's crust. By close observation of a beach it is possible to see in miniature, over a period of hours or days or seasons, some of the kinds of geologic processes that over periods of millions of years are molding mountain ranges and altering the shapes of continents. The river of sand makes deposits along its edges, adding to the size of beaches, bars, and spits. At other times the surf cuts away sand and diminishes the size of the beaches, occasionally causing havoc in built-up areas where men ignorant of the processes of nature have disobeyed the biblical injunction against houses built on sand.

Watch the beach closely through the seasons and you will notice that normally it is much wider and higher in the summer and fall than in the spring and winter. The seasonal difference arises from the varying behavior of the ocean. The gentle waves of summer and fall, carrying sand in suspension, wash up on the shore and deposit their load, adding to the beach. But when the storms come up in November and December the waves have considerably more speed and power. As they wash up higher on the beach, the backwash is faster, and the swiftly flowing water is able to carry away sand that was dropped by the slower waves of summer.

Sometimes the "berm," the main upper part of the beach where the sunbathers congregate, is entirely cut away, and waves wash over the entire beach. At Ocean Beach the storm waves sometimes batter the sea wall. But the summertime beach extends as much as one hundred and thirty feet farther seaward than the winter beach. A berm twelve feet high in the summer has been entirely destroyed by an early winter storm surf. Although a sizable berm may be built up over a period of many months, it can be entirely destroyed by waves in the course of a single violent storm.

Even more noticeable than the seasonal changes at Ocean Beach are the changes in the small "pocket beaches" along the Golden Gate. There the changes can easily be measured in reference to the surrounding rocks. During the summer and early fall there are a good many pocket beaches in the small coves between the promontories at the foot of the Presidio, Sea Cliff, and Lincoln Park. But their days are numbered. During the first winter storms they may entirely disappear and the rocks beneath the sand will lie completely exposed. If the winter is mild, however, they may remain through the year. Sometimes a pocket beach may remain through a series of mild winters only to be destroyed by a single storm, exposing rocks that have not been visible for many years, or perhaps decades.

Thus, in addition to yearly cycles in beach development, there are both shorter cycles, varying from tide to tide, and longer cycles, varying from decade to decade. There is a point on the south shore of the Golden Gate at Land's End where you can still see at low tide some of the remains of

the tanker *Lyman Stewart*, which ran aground here in 1922. For some time
after the ship was wrecked it could be reached at low tide by simply walking
over the sand, and the hulk was so accessible it was used as a lodging place
by hobos until it was broken up by the continual battering of the waves.
In recent years there has been no sand in sight, and the remains of the
ship, some twenty yards offshore, are surrounded by deep water. The phenomenon may have been an example of a beach created by artificial means.
The wrecked ship, acting as a breakwater, protected the immediate shore
from the direct impact of the large waves. The waves that did reach the shore
inside the "breakwater" were so diminished in size and speed as to deposit
the sand they otherwise would have held in suspension, creating a beach
that was eventually built all the way out to the ship. Over the years, as the
wreck was disintegrated by the power of the surf, the breakwater was elim-
inated and the beach it had created was washed away. Some of the wreckage
visible here is from the tanker *Frank H. Buck*, which piled up at this point
in 1937.

A particularly good place to watch seasonal changes along the shore is
on the outer Golden Gate at the mouth of Lobos Creek on Bakers Beach,
where the water of the small stream combines with the force of the waves
to create striking effects—miniature sand bars, islands, peninsulas, and sand
cliffs. The course of the stream and the contours of the beach may change
over a period of hours in ways comparable to changes that occur over a
period of years or decades at the mouths of large rivers.

At certain times, particularly during the summer and fall when there is
little or no surf, the stream will flow directly into the Golden Gate. Higher
waves will tend to build a sand bar across the mouth, forcing the stream
to curve some distance to the southwest. The semimonthly spring tides
or storm waves may break through the sand bar and carve small vertical
embankments. In the winter of 1959–60 a heavy storm and high waves
created at the creek's mouth an impressive sand cliff fifteen feet high and
more than a hundred yards long. At Ocean Beach waves from the same
storm, coming with a gale from the south, undercut the sea wall below the
Cliff House, revealing the wall's foundation, which had not been visible in
many years.

Shoreline observers have often been puzzled by the question of what
happens during the winter to the sand that is removed from the beaches

by storm waves. Part of the sand is evidently held in suspension in the sand river and a larger portion is deposited on the ocean bottom beneath the river. There it remains in a kind of winter hibernation, awaiting summer. Most of it seems to be deposited offshore where the water is about twelve feet deep. The waves, stirring the bottom even at that depth, continually tend to move the sand toward shore, but the backwash of the big winter combers is sufficient to counterbalance that tendency and prevent the sand from being deposited on the beach. In the summer, when the waves diminish in size, the shoreward movement of the sand exceeds the backwash, and the beach is built up again.

The Mystery of the Great Bar

Off the Golden Gate the submarine sand moves in ways that are not well understood. The movements are determined, evidently, by the complex interaction of conflicting waves and currents. When the swells from far storms are rolling in toward the coast or the ocean surface is roughened by wind, a mile or two off Point Bonita (the northern head of the Golden Gate) the waves crest into foam and the surface is roiled into white water. Mariners call this zone of turbulence the Potato Patch and warily steer clear. (A dubious legend holds that coastal schooners used to lose their deckloads of potatoes while rolling in the rough water here.) Sometimes at low tides the uproar is not confined to the Potato Patch but extends in a giant half circle for some eleven miles outside the Golden Gate, visible from the air or the upper slopes of Tamalpais. The choppy surface marks the location of the Great Bar, a perilous barrier to ships since the days of the Forty-Niners and a geological phenomenon that may be a clue to long-term changes in the crust of the earth hereabouts.

The depth of the ocean on either side of the bar ranges up to ninety feet, but there is less than forty feet of water over the bar at low tide. The Potato Patch appears over the shallowest part of the bar, the Four Fathom Bank, which rises to within twenty-three feet of the surface. Here, when the tide is extremely low and the swells high, there may be scarcely enough water in the troughs to float a surfboard. The principal ship entrance through the bar is the Main Channel, at the outermost point of the semicircle, maintained by dredging to a depth of fifty feet and marked by a series of channel buoys.

Nobody knows precisely why the Great Bar is there. Geologists will only speculate about the mystery. Their guesses involve not only the peculiar motion of the currents through the Golden Gate but the shape of this coastline a million years ago. One explanation is that the Great Bar is simply a variation of the kind of sand barrier that the ocean normally builds across the entrance to bays and lagoons as an extension of coastal beaches in the direction of the prevailing currents. The sandspit extending from Stinson Beach to Bolinas, north of the Golden Gate, and a similar spit at Drake's Bay, farther up the coast, are examples of the conventional kind of bar.

Under this explanation, the Great Bar, an extension of San Francisco's Ocean Beach, would be a dam of sand directly across the entrance to the Golden Gate if it were not for the power of the currents ebbing outward through the strait, bulging the bar into its peculiar horseshoe shape.

Yet this theory raises several questions. Why is the Great Bar asymmetrical, with one end immediately north of the Golden Gate and the other some three miles south? And if the outgoing tides are strong enough to push the bar seaward, why wouldn't flood currents, on the incoming tides, exert equal pressure in the opposite direction, keeping the sand in place directly across the Gate entrance as it does across the entrances to other bays and lagoons?

A second theory is that the bar is composed at least partly of sediments carried by the rivers emptying into the bay, primarily the waters of the Sacramento and San Joaquin, draining the Central Valley and the Sierra Nevada, a sixty-thousand-square-mile area about the size of New England. Thus within the bar could be silt from the orchards of the Sacramento Valley or tailings from the gold fields of the Mother Lode. This story seems plausible when you look seaward from the slopes of Tamalpais after heavy rains and see the ocean stained brown for miles offshore by the silt-laden river waters flowing out the Golden Gate.

This explanation seems contradicted by the findings of the Army Corps of Engineers, concerned with dredging channels for shipping. The engineers have discovered that the bar is composed mainly not of silt but much heavier particles of sand. And they believe the sand could not be deposited there by the Sacramento-San Joaquin, which drops most of its sandy load long before it reaches the Golden Gate, in the relatively quiet waters of Suisun and San Pablo bays. The currents carry out to sea the fine silt that is not heavy enough to sink to the bottom of the bay en route to the ocean. Some of the silt flows back inside the Golden Gate when the tide shifts, and is deposited on the bay floor, creating deep layers of bay mud. Other silt evidently sinks to the ocean floor beyond the bar, but the currents across the top of the bar, the engineers believe, are swift enough to prevent its being deposited there.

A third explanation for the existence of the Great Bar is even more intriguing. The bar, in this theory, is the remnant of an ancient land form created in past geologic ages when the Golden Gate was young and San Francisco Bay had not yet come into existence. Picture here, where the bay is now located, a valley threaded by a major river, the Sacramento-San Joaquin, flowing in from the northeast, cutting two gorges through the rising hills bounding the valley. One of the gorges is now the strait of Carquinez; the other is the Golden Gate. This was the scene at the end of the late Pleistocene epoch, some fifteen thousand to twenty-five thousand years ago, when much of the earth's water was contained in the glaciers. Sea level was close to four hundred feet lower than at present, and the coastline was far to the west of the present shore. The river flowed into the ocean at some point west of the Golden Gate, possibly beyond the Farallones, twenty-five miles offshore. There it deposited its load of sediment, forming a broad delta. The waves of the ocean battered away at the delta and at the ancient shoreline, forming beaches. Giant winds drifted the sand inland and piled it into vast dunes, similar to those which in historical times covered the western part of San Francisco.

As the last Ice Age came to an end in a big thaw some eight thousand to fifteen thousand years ago, the glaciers melted and the sea level rose. The dunes of the old delta and the ancient shoreline were gradually submerged by the rising waters, and the higher dunes were shaped by waves and currents into a big semicircle. This, then, according to the third theory, is the San Francisco Bar, a relic of the Ice Age, a time of frigid climate and a shrunken sea.

Recent studies at the University of California's Hydraulic Engineering Laboratory seem to support the Ice Age theory, with one major exception:

The sand on top of the bar seems to come from inside the bay. Geologist D. B. Moore discovered a previously unknown channel of sand between the Golden Gate and Carquinez. The mineral content of some of the bar sands matched that of the sands in the bay and even of rock formations far up the Sacramento River and its tributaries. Yet the sand from the ocean floor around the bar, at depths below sixty feet, is of different mineral composition, similar to that of rock formations some distance north of the Golden Gate.

To explain the different origins of the shallower and the deeper sands, Moore went back to the Ice Age theory. When the coastline was out near the Farallones, the waves from the northwest brought beach sands down from the north coast in a persistent longshore drift. As the sea rose to near its present level, submerging the old delta with its beaches and the dunes, the waves, which had been eroding a straight coastal plain, began to cut into the base of the Coast Range, creating headlands and embayments. The headlands, jutting seaward like breakwaters, cut off most of the wave-transported sand from the sources north along the shore. Very little sand reaches the bar nowadays from the northern coast.

The bar itself, then, has evidently been laid down on the top of the Ice Age sands by the powerful sediment-bearing waters from the Golden Gate. It is possible to offer tentative answers to some of the questions raised about the bar. The problem as to why the south end of the bar is three miles from the Golden Gate may be a matter of the ocean currents. At the Main Channel, for example, there seems to be a prevailing northerly current, which could push the bar south of where it otherwise would be. As to the question of why the bar bulges seaward rather than extending directly across the mouth of the Gate, the explanation may lie in the funneling effect of the Gate on the ebb tide. The powerful, turbid, ebbing waters of the bay are confined to the narrow strait through which the water flows as it would through a nozzle, with far more force than could be exerted by the slowly rising flood tide. The nozzle effect keeps the bar far offshore.

But there are still many aspects of the bar that are unexplained. What is its relation to Ocean Beach, for example? If the sands of Ocean Beach come principally from the cliffs to the south and move northward on a longshore current, why doesn't that same current push the south end of the bar closer to the Gate? And is there any interchange between the beach and bar sands, particularly at the point where the bar is in contact with the beach?

The answers—and the questions as to which of the several explanations of the bar's existence is most valid—must await still more research. Meantime the layman can watch the sea over the bar roil into white during the winter storms and devise his own theories as to the origin of this peculiar land form, the largest single geographical feature within the city limits.

Assault from the Sea

The two most spectacular shows that take place regularly in San Francisco are never reviewed in the newspapers. One is the march of the summer fog when it moves in low through the Golden Gate and down the leeward slopes of the coastal hills. The other is the spectacle of the breaking surf along the western and northern margins of the city. In no other major city in the United States—and in few if any others in the world—is it possible to see such varied and magnificent displays of oceanic pyrotechnics as are visible along the five miles of Ocean Beach and the beaches and cliffs of the Golden Gate. One reason is the city's location directly on the open coast of the Pacific. The prevailing westerlies—a belt of winds blowing from the west around the world in the middle latitudes—move across the Pacific toward this coast, piling up high waves, then continue inland across the continent to the East Coast and out to sea, in opposition to the waves coming ashore from the Atlantic, tending to flatten them out. As a result, the waves on this coast are consistently far larger and more powerful than those of the eastern seaboard.

There are two principal kinds of surf waves, with innumerable gradations between. The most common kind can be seen along Ocean Beach on almost any day; they have been whipped up by the onshore breezes and race toward the beach in quick succession. The water is choppy, and the waves seldom attain a large size. The prime breakers, however, are more rare; they originate in storms far at sea. The farther away the storm, the longer the interval between the waves. A period of five seconds or more between waves indicates a distant origin. Although there have been few adequate measurements of waves off San Francisco, giant waves rolling ashore at Long Beach on one occasion were clocked at an amazing thirty seconds between crests, indicating that they had probably originated somewhere in the Southern Hemisphere.

Often the waves arrive in series called "wave trains"—several big ones followed by several smaller ones or by an interval of almost flat water. Within each train the size may increase until the largest is followed by a period of relative calm before the next series arrives. The legend that the biggest wave is always the ninth one—or the seventh or the fifth—is pure fiction. The number and size of waves in each series depend on many variables, including the effect of opposite-moving trains they have encountered in their journey over hundreds or thousands of miles of ocean.

South of the Cliff House as far as you can see on a clear day, long lines of breakers often churn the water into white for two hundred yards or more offshore. This is one of the world's most dramatic surfs. Yet the very gradual slope of the bottom, causing the waves to break far out, makes it impossible to observe closely the critical breaking point from any position on the beach. When a high surf is running, the Cliff House area is the best accessible place from which to see the display of wave-bursts on rocks, both on the cliffs immediately below and on Seal Rocks just offshore. But to observe the pure form of the breaking wave, the unparalleled beauty of the moving water uncomplicated by interference from offshore rocks, go to Bakers Beach on the outer Golden Gate.

Although this beach is partly protected by the heads of the Gate at Point Lobos and Point Bonita and the breakers are consequently not as large as those at Ocean Beach, the bottom slopes more rapidly offshore and the waves break much closer to the beach, often not more than twenty to thirty yards out. Very large waves are the exception here: Padre Pedro Font, who explored this beach with Anza in 1776, noted that the water was very calm and thought it would be a good place for small boats to come ashore from their ships. But I have seen many days at Bakers Beach when no one in his senses would think of running a boat through the surf.

During a high surf, the rollers from the far storms appear first offshore as barely discernible swells that rise as they ride up over an increasingly shallow bottom. Slowly each swell grows until its front steepens and darkens in shadow. Still it continues to rise, as if with an anticipatory roll of drums. Small flecks of white may appear at the top and quickly merge like a

43

dancing flame racing along the crest. For an interminable moment the crest rises higher and higher, becoming intolerably top-heavy. The base of the wave, slowed by the frictional drag of the ocean floor, can no longer move as fast as the top. The critical instant has arrived.

At this point the crest of the wave may be twelve feet or more above the trough immediately ahead. When the tide is high on this beach the critical instant arrives more quickly than it would otherwise. The water from a previous wave, having reached a point high up on the steep beach, comes charging seaward again in a massive backwash that continues across the shallows and rolls out to meet the oncoming wave. It slaps against the cresting swell with an impact that sends sheets of water leaping several feet farther into the air. Then, obeying a law of physics that this wave watcher has never been able to comprehend, the two waves pass entirely through each other. The backwash spends itself seaward, but for the incoming wave the moment of crisis has arrived, triggered by the impact. The white crest topples forward and with a long leap arches out in advance of the base, propelled by the accumulated power of the massed waters behind it. For a single wondrous point in time, the upper masses of water seem to be suspended there in the most fantastically beautiful curve in all inanimate nature, the white crest curling forward, the body of the wave below it now for one fraction of a second a translucent emerald in the sun.

Often this perfect curve of green water pulls into it some of the marbled foam of a previous breaker, drawing the white up into the hollow of the wave where it accentuates the curve, streaking the arching emerald like filaments of spun wool. Then the arch of the crest is completed, and tons of white water hit the surface ahead with a reverberating thunderclap that volleys along the entire front as other sectors of the wave, variously affected by the differences in the ocean floor, plunge forward a second or two apart. After the impact comes the rebound. Raging masses of white rise again and leap forward toward the shore.

Sometimes another impressive effect takes place. Immediately after the upward rebound, as the leading masses of white water are falling again, a battery of geysers shoots toward the sky from the rear of the turbulent zone. Evidently some part of the forward-arching crest, instead of rebounding from the flat surface, continued the downward curve, hit the bottom, and now rises again to spout high in the rear of the comber. Under extraordinary conditions these geysers shoot up from ten to twenty feet, with the spray of occasional jets perhaps reaching thirty feet. When this geyser effect takes place at Bakers Beach along a front of several hundred yards, rising against a backdrop of the dark Marin hills on the far shore, complemented by the urgent upward thrust of the red towers of the Golden Gate Bridge, the spectacle reaches its climax.

After the break, the race is on. As the comber charges toward the beach, separate salients of the wave front leap a short distance ahead with an extra burst of speed only to be overtaken and passed by others. Ultimately the wave reaches shallow water, is slowed by the backwash of previous waves, and spreads itself thin, particularly at low tide when the beach is flat. Then the white of the foam and the brown of the sand stirred from the bottom combine to produce a smooth marbled surface that spreads over flat acres of shore in evolving curves and merging shapes that sink at last into the beach or recede to become part of the next breaker. The sound—which began with a barely discernible rumble, exploded into a thunderclap, and continued with the roar and din of moving masses of water—subsides in a diminuendo of watery hissings and splashings, rises again on the backwash, and merges into the explosion of the next breaking wave.

And so the spectacle continues, wave after wave repeating the basic form yet creating innumerable variations of size, sound, shape and motion, cycle after cycle, like something rolling out of the beginning of time and receding again to become part of an unknowable future. The waves arriving here daily at the city's doorstep are the visible symbols of the basic rhythms of the earth—the rolling waters, the rising tides, the cyclonic storms and the rivers of air that flow across the face of the planet.

The Green Ridge

Throughout the city there are other symbols of the rhythms of the earth— the infinitely slower rhythms of the land itself, moving over a period of millions of years as the ocean surface moves in a few seconds. One such symbol is the belt of serpentine that extends diagonally across the city from southeast to northwest, along the zone of the Hunters Point-Fort Point Fault. Study, for example, the outcrop on which the U. S. Mint stands, at Market and Duboce. Here, as elsewhere, the serpentine is a striking gray-green in color, often soft, as rocks go, with hard blocks surrounded by crumbly material that breaks easily along the slick, shiny planes which the ancients thought resembled the tough smooth hide of a serpent.

Serpentine is a source of jade, and it contains magnesium, mercury, asbestos, chromite, and nickel, though not here in commercial quantities. The rock's texture makes it sometimes useful as jewelry or as building facing. It glistens like green glass when the light strikes it from certain angles, and it is particularly luminous after it is washed by rain.

It is no coincidence that in the city the serpentine occurs almost entirely in the Hunters Point-Fort Point Fault zone. This is the kind of rock that was once plastic and was pressured from below into crustal cracks or weak zones, entering not in a hot molten state, like granite or lava, but cool and semisolid, like fudge on a sundae. Rising from below, or possibly from some side angle, it would tend to invade areas of low resistance, such as rock that had been fragmented by recurrent grinding along a fault. It was for this reason that geologist Julius Schlocker detected the existence of the Hunters Point-Fort Point Fault when he found serpentine extending in a narrow zone across the city, containing fragments of sandstone picked up en route.

Despite its frequent softness, serpentine seems to be relatively resistant to erosion (mainly owing to its impervious nature) and it remains as hills or high outcrops like that at the Mint, after surrounding rocks have been worn down. Consequently the serpentine forms a discontinuous ridge or series of high points across the city—not as high as those formed by the harder and more resistant chert, but in a series of low hills, beginning with Hunters Point, where it underlies the housing project and other areas on the hill. Immediately northwest, Potrero Hill is almost entirely serpentine, causing problems to home gardeners, owing to the infertility of soil derived from it. Driving north on the James Lick Freeway, you can see the Potrero serpentine near San Francisco Hospital at about the point where the downtown area comes into view as the road slices a flank of the hill.

Northwest of Potrero Hill the serpentine disappears beneath filled areas of the Mission district and recurs where the University of California Extension campus rises above the valley of Market Street just west of the Freeway overpass. Here it appears, as elsewhere in San Francisco, as a part of a mixture with other kinds of rock fragments, mainly sandstone.

The ridge continues northwest to Alamo Square and then to Anza Vista and the high ground around Sears, Roebuck and on to Laurel Hill, site of the glassy Fireman's Fund building. Serpentine is found at nearby Lone Mountain and the University of San Francisco. The long serpentine ridge extends to the Presidio and is readily visible in a quarry below the Arguello lookout point.

The biggest display of all is below the Presidio in the cliffs of the Golden Gate, where over the millenniums the tidal currents have cut deep into the bedrock that underlies the city. You can see exposures in cross sections along the road to Fort Point and in the cliffs behind the fort. At some points along the hazardous and well-nigh inaccessible shoreline southwest of the bridge there are massive cliffs of the green rock, landslides of slick serpentine soil, oozy gelatinous masses where ground water has invaded the rock, boulders of many sizes varying in texture and in color from pale olive to a rich jade, sometimes veined with thin white filaments or studded with tiny smooth facets that reflect gemlike points of light. Under certain angles of illumination, particularly at sunset, the green rock glitters along the shore like the Emerald City of Oz.

Here the serpentine extends not only high overhead but deep into the earth beneath the floor of the Golden Gate. The south tower of the bridge was built on serpentine, setting off the renowned intermural battle of the bearded geologists. Just prior to construction Professor Bailey Willis of Stanford objected vociferously that the bridge was to be built on "weak serpentine puddingstone," while Professor Andrew Lawson of the University of California, official consultant to the bridge builders, insisted that the rock was solid. The controversy was complicated by the fact that there are many kinds of serpentine, ranging from the more common crumbly sheared variety to massive outcrops as hard as granite. Certain changes were made in the foundation, however, and further pressure tests quieted the controversy, although Willis to the end of his life maintained that "only time will tell."

Deep Lagoon

Some of the land forms of the city are not so easily explained as the belt of serpentine, and geologists are not certain about their origin. One of them is visible along Seventh Avenue, where it becomes the only through road between Twin Peaks and Golden Gate Heights, following an old trail at the foot of the mountain. Near Laguna Honda reservoir the road traverses the narrow Laguna Honda canyon; to the east are the lower slopes of Twin Peaks and Mount Sutro and to the west a peculiar hundred-foot cliff of sand.

Why there should be a sand cliff at this point, nobody knows. The slope, although not vertical, seems far too steep to be a normal sand-dune contour. The sand was obviously brought by the wind up from the beach across the dunes of the Sunset district. It surmounted the six-hundred-foot ridge of Golden Gate Heights and drifted down the east side of the ridge. Just leeward of the ridge there is a built-over shelf a quarter of a mile wide where the sand is relatively level before suddenly dropping off to the Laguna Honda canyon.

One theory for the existence of this odd cliff is simply that the sand follows the contours of the underlying bedrock. This theory is plausible, but it fails to explain why there would be such a cliff in the bedrock at this point. Cliffs are abnormalities in any landscape, and are usually formed either by faulting or by the cutting action of moving water, as along a seacoast or riverbank. The Laguna Honda cliff could scarcely be an earth-quake fault; a drop in the terrain great enough to leave a hundred-foot escarpment would extend over a much longer area and disrupt the land-scape visibly for miles. And it could not have been cut by wave action even if the ocean had once been this high, four hundred feet above present sea level. A seacliff would face the sea, not a mountain.

The only explanation left seems to be the most credible. A swiftly moving stream could have undercut the bank, carved an escarpment (which was later covered by sand), and carried away any surplus sand that drifted down the slope into it, maintaining the steepness of the cliff. The cliff curves slightly as a stream would curve. And such a stream would have drained a good-sized watershed on the west side of Twin Peaks. But there are bugs in this theory. The steepest part of the cliff is opposite the Laguna Honda (Deep Lagoon) reservoir, a natural lake before it was dammed and enlarged as a source of the city's water supply a century ago. The cliff would have been carved by running water, not still water.

Moreover, about two hundred yards north of the reservoir, near the intersection of Seventh Avenue and Lawton, there was another natural lake, filled in in the early years of this century. It was about the same elevation as Laguna Honda. The stream flowing between them could not have been very swift. And there is no indication as to where any substantial stream might have gone. There is no ravine below or any indication of a streambed that would have carried the amount of water necessary to have carved such a cliff. Where the streambed might have been, there is nothing but sand. Yet in that fact we may have a clue as to what actually took place. Conceivably a swift stream could have carved the cliff, then later been dammed by landslides, creating lagoons.

Remember that not so long ago, geologically speaking, sea level was far below its present elevation, possibly as much as four hundred feet lower. When the shoreline was still some miles farther west than at present, the drifting sand from the beach probably did not reach so far inland as the Laguna Honda area. The cliff in Laguna Honda canyon could have been carved by the stream at that time. With lower sea level, the gradient of the stream flowing down to the sea would have been steep, causing it to flow fast enough to create such a cliff at the point where the water was confined between the lower slopes of Twin Peaks on the east and Golden Gate Heights on the west. Then, as sea level rose toward its present height, the stream would have flowed more slowly and the drifting sand would have reached it to dam it up, create the lagoons, and fill the ravine it had carved downstream.

If this theory is correct, we may expect that the old stream canyon is out there someplace beneath the sand, possibly following the general line of Golden Gate Park to the beach and continuing beneath the ocean sands to the ancient sea level line. In this theory, too, we have an explanation of most of the city's other natural impoundments of water—Lake Merced, Pine Lake, the Chain of Lakes in the park, and possibly Mountain Lake. They may occupy canyons carved by Ice Age streams running swiftly down to a far lower sea level. Rising sea level at the end of the Ice Age slowed the course of the streams, and as the beach advanced eastward its sands drifted into the old canyons, damming them and impounding their waters to form the present lakes.

Before the city was built, there were lakes and lagoons around the bayward shores as well. Father Font's diary of 1776 describes a large one along the northern slopes below Pacific Heights, in the Cow Hollow area, probably the one that became known in Gold Rush times as Washerwoman's Lagoon,

49

just west of Van Ness. He also mentions two lagoons in what may have been the Market Street and Hayes Valley districts, and the most famous of all, Laguna de los Dolores, from which Mission Dolores took its name. (Font notes that the "Arroyo de los Dolores" issued from Twin Peaks by way of a waterfall, which evidently was near the upper end of Eighteenth Street.) Probably these lagoons, too, occupied old valleys carved during the Ice Age by steeper streams in a period of lower sea level.

The Beach on the Hill

Among the diverse land forms of the city there are puzzling pieces of geologic evidence that do not seem to fit neatly into the picture of a steadily rising sea level. At one point in the Presidio is a strange feature that seems to indicate that sea level was once much higher in relation to the land. In 1952 geologists probing in an excavation for the Presidio housing development off Lincoln Boulevard about one hundred feet above the level of Bakers Beach discovered several acres of sand that did not resemble the dune sand that had drifted up from the beach.

Dune sand normally is deposited in beds that curve with the shape of the dune, but the beds in this deposit were flat, sloping slightly toward Bakers Beach. This deposit bore all the marks of beach sand deposited by waves. But how could waves have deposited sand one hundred feet above sea level? There is evidence that during an interglacial period some hundred thousand years ago, when there was less polar ice than at present, sea level may have been about sixty feet higher than it is now. There is also evidence that the Coast Range, of which San Francisco is a part, has been rising sporadically. Conceivably this sand could have been the remains of an ancient beach laid down by the waves at a time when the land surface was lower and sea level higher.

On the peninsula south of San Francisco there is evidence that seems to bear out this theory—a broad, flat marine terrace planed off by the waves. This is the wide shelf on which coastal towns are built and which is followed by California State Highway 1. The shelf is roughly one hundred feet above sea level—about the same height as the odd sand deposit in the Presidio. This "hundred-foot terrace" appears also at Bolinas and other points to the north. Evidently the terrace and the "old beach" at the Presidio were formed at about the same time, before the land rose and the sea level fell.

On the other hand, there are oddly no signs of the terrace in the Presidio or anywhere in San Francisco. In fact many geologists believe that the land around San Francisco has not risen recently but subsided, pointing to the existence of the bay as evidence. Certainly this is the lowest part of the entire Coast Range. One explanation for the absence of the terrace here is that local subsidence may have lowered the terrace to sea level, or below. But if this theory is correct, how is it possible to account for a beach so far above sea level? Even more difficult to explain is the fact that the sands of this old beach do not have the appearance of ancient, weathered sands but seem almost as fresh as sands laid down by the ocean daily on Bakers Beach below. Possibly some day geologists probing the Presidio will come across new clues that will throw light on the existence of this beach one hundred feet in the air. Until then, its origin remains unknown, affording intriguing material for speculation by geologists and laymen alike, a symbol of the mysteries attending the rising and falling of the earth's crust over the eons of geologic time.

Huge blocks of radiolarian chert in Sutro Forest resemble the ruins of some ancient temple in the jungle. The inch-thick beds in some places dip to the east in conformity with the bedrock of much of Mount Sutro; in other areas the beds are vertical where big slabs of the rock wall have broken off and fallen. The dark red and orange colors of the chert contrast with the greens and grays of lichens growing on the rock, and the colors change as the moving light filters through the leaves of eucalyptus and cypress.

Chert beds laid down on the bottom of an ancient sea millions of years ago now rise above the city from Tank Hill and Mount Olympus, eastern spurs of Twin Peaks. Thin layers of shale are sandwiched between the chert beds.

West of Twin Peaks is a long north-south ridge about seven hundred feet high known as Sunset Heights or Golden Gate Heights, composed principally of chert. Near Fourteenth Avenue and Ortega are high cliffs of chert, mixed here and there with volcanic rock, forming a long escarpment with caves and revealing admirable natural carvings and contorted beds. Monterey cypresses grow at the north end on the city's highest dune, where the sand from Ocean Beach has drifted over the chert.

At Quarry Lake in Golden Gate Park, ivy and gnarled roots of Monterey pine frame outcrops of the bedded chert beneath the sand that covers most of the park.

Chert outcrops in Glen Canyon, below Diamond Heights, offer good training facilities for aspiring rock climbers. The chert layers provide the kind of footholds essential to rope work.

Volcanic greenstone is found in the city's central block along with chert. Although both rocks are often dark red, greenstone is readily distinguished from the layered chert because it tends to be unlayered or massive. On Corona Heights a greenstone outcrop looms against a backdrop of Nob Hill, from the Comstock on the left to the Mark Hopkins on the right.

On Golden Gate Heights greenstone lies directly above the stratified chert in a particularly well-defined meeting of the two kinds of rock above a bed of sweet alyssum.

At one point along the cliffs of Golden Gate there is a striking juxtaposition of the two principal kinds of bedrock underlying the city. In an area composed principally of sandstone, a narrow ridge of chert juts seaward just northeast of a sandstone point. The waves rush into a small cove between them, eroding the fault that separates the two kinds of rock. The light-gray sandstone is massive but seamed; the maroon-colored chert is in steeply angled beds that dip to the north, away from the sandstone. On one side of the chert ridge are the jagged edges of upended beds; on the other the back of the dipping beds presents a smoother appearance, resembling overlapping slabs an inch or two thick.

At Fort Funston are still remnants of the kind of dunes that lie beneath the Richmond and Sunset districts and once constituted the Great Sand Waste west of Twin Peaks. Planted on the dunes to hold the sand are the kinds of beach grasses sown by William Hammond Hall and John McLaren to make Golden Gate Park possible.

Partly covered by ice plant and wild oats is the city's highest dune on Golden Gate Heights, where the wind carried sand as high as six hundred feet above sea level. Tracks indicate an abundance of animal life in the dunes.

Unnoticed alongside a cliff-top trail, embedded in a sandbank, are shells evidently denoting the site of an Indian encampment. The shell mound, uncovered by drifting sands, may be hundreds of years old.

The sandy beds in the cliffs at Fort Funston are part of the Colma formation, laid down during a period ten thousand to five hundred thousand years ago. Compare these beds with those of current beach deposits at the mouth of Lobos Creek on Bakers Beach, pictured on page 76. During the Colma period sea level was higher in relation to the land; San Francisco's hills were islands; and the area pictured here was the bottom or beach of a channel that ran from the ocean inland along the south side of the San Bruno range. The Colma sands were laid down on top of the Merced formation (pictured on page 80) which in turn was deposited on top of the ancient Franciscan formation.

The exposed beds on Golden Gate Heights are far higher, standing at elevations of six hundred and seven hundred feet above sea level, and could not have been deposited by the ocean. They consist of dune sand, blown to this height by sea winds in an uninterrupted sweep from Ocean Beach, two miles to the west. Beneath the sand is bedrock of Franciscan chert, a barrier around which the sand was piled by the wind.

As waves from the open ocean roll beneath the Golden Gate Bridge, they are slowed by friction from contact with the shoaling bottom near the shoreline, become top-heavy, break and batter the century-old sea wall at Fort Point.

Off the Cliff House, summer and winter, intrepid surfers gauge with expert eye the rising ridges of water, the crests of foam, the light in the hollow of the curling combers, and, with luck, feel beneath their feet the swelling power of the ocean's edge.

The fisherman at Land's End may catch no fish, but he is a participant in a grand show of the rhythms of the breaking waves.

Storm waves at Land's End present innumerable variations of form and power as backwash and crosscurrents shape the form of each break and the wind rips long banners of spindrift from the plunging crests.

The power of the surf attacking the edge of the land is nowhere more dramatically illustrated than in the remains of ships that have gone aground and been battered to pieces by the waves. Off Land's End near Mile Rock, visible at low tide, are the remains of the *Frank H. Buck,* an oil tanker that was disabled by a collision with the liner *President Coolidge* in 1937 and drifted ashore here, oddly enough at the same spot that the tanker's sister ship, the *Lyman Stewart,* had run aground in 1922.

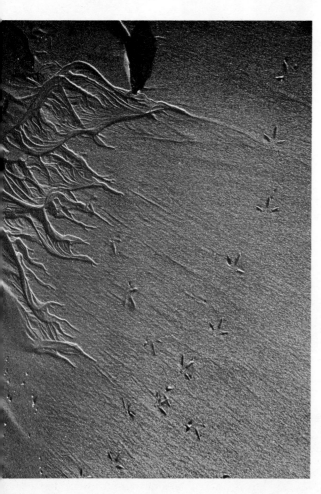

As the tide recedes, the exposed sand is a *tabula rasa*, on which is written the calligraphy of the moving waters and of shorebirds. For some unknown reason the sheet of water leaves an intricate backwash record of diamond-shaped markings and herringbone patterns, providing, as in the scene below at Bakers Beach, an arresting contrast with the curves of the breaking waves, the long headland of Point Bonita, the high ridge of Tamalpais, and the vapory shapes of cumulus clouds.

During the interval of low tide, water that has sunk into the higher part of the beach during the previous high tide seeps out at lower points and flows down the slope of the hard flat sand, creating miniature river patterns called rill marks. Usually the rill marks are scarcely more than a quarter-inch thick, but sometimes on steeper beaches, such as this beach at Land's End, they may reach the depth of small gullies.

At Fort Funston, the rill marks reflect the "badland" patterns of wrinkles and gullies in the cliffs.

At the bottom of the cliffs along the shore of the Golden Gate, battering waves undermine cliffs and boulders, causing huge fragments to split off and fall, forming jagged edges.

But in time the persistent action of the waves wears away the sharp edges and shapes the rocks into smooth, swelling, sculptured forms pleasant to the touch as well as to the sight.

A hike along the beaches of the Golden Gate at low tide may reveal an intriguing flotsam left by the waves—timbers from wave-beaten pilings, redwood logs that washed from the northern coast after a flood, driftwood of all sizes and shapes, floats from fishermen's nets, the shell remains of crustaceans, the half-destroyed body of a big pelican, or even fragments of broken monuments dumped over the sea cliff. The partly legible inscription on the granite stone reads:

In the Year 1847 at Clar . . .
Where Broadway Crosses Ba . . .
Wharf in San Francisco Bay . . .

The stone is evidently part of a memorial to William Squire Clark, who in 1847 built the city's first wharf at Clark's Point, where Broadway crossed Battery. The memorial stood in the old Laurel Hill Cemetery, near California and Presidio. In an incredible act of official vandalism which destroyed the burial places of many of San Francisco's pioneers, the graveyard was ripped up in the 1930s, the remains were removed, and the stones dumped over the cliff into the waters of the Golden Gate.

Phelan Beach is a pocket of sand below the mansions of the Seacliff district, where summer fog often drifts in and out among the Monterey pines. This is still "China Beach" to old-timers, who tell of the era when Chinese fishermen camped here.

The gentle waves of summer deposit sand and build beaches; the powerful waves of winter cut away sand and destroy beaches. This huge, multiple-rooted eucalyptus log was deposited in a cove at the northeast end of Bakers Beach by a high winter surf and almost completely buried by the beach-building waves of summer.

The following winter, swift storm waves cut away the sands around it, leaving it looking as if the heads of trapped animals were protruding from the sand. Finally the sand was completely removed, and after the last picture was taken winter waves picked up the log and deposited it a quarter mile down the beach. The depth of sand in this cove may vary as much as fifteen feet between winter and summer. The surrounding rocks are sandstone.

On a minus tide and a low surf you can
walk or wade below the Cliff House,
and on extremely rare occasions, when
the waves have deposited exactly the
right amount of sand, you can explore
caves and tunnels deep in the cliff.

7 4

Seal Rocks, off the Cliff House, are "sea stacks," massive sandstone that was once part of the mainland and became isolated as the attacks of waves over thousands of years destroyed the less-resistant rock around them. They illustrate the retreat of the shoreline, which was previously far west of its present location. The arch visible below was produced by the kind of wave action at work in the top picture. Eventually the entire stack will be reduced to sea level by wave attack.

The best place to see rapid changes in a landscape is on Bakers Beach at the point where Lobos Creek joins the waters of Golden Gate and illustrates in microcosm the processes that are shaping the crust of the earth. The form of the beach changes with each tide in response to waves and the fresh-water runoff, which daily carve new escarpments and form miniature grand canyons. The strata are laid down not by millennial sedimentation but by the advance and retreat of the tidal waters.

High waves on a high tide tend to deposit only larger, lighter colored grains; the lower, more slowly moving waves drop finer, darker colored grains, resulting in the striations visible in the sand cliffs.

Storm waves may remove several vertical feet of sand in a day. Thus in a few hours changes occur here that take place in larger landscapes only over periods of hundreds or thousands of years.

The sandstone bedrock that underlies much of the city is revealed at Land's End and at Telegraph Hill. Geologists call it "graywacke"; its natural color is gray, although weathering turns it to light brown and ultimately to pale orange, also causing it in time to become soft and crumbly.

A honeycomb effect in sandstone at the Presidio cliffs is produced by differences in the kind of "glue" that cements the grains of sand together. Some of the cementing material is less resistant to wind and waves and disintegrates sooner, leaving the holes, surrounded by ridges and surfaces bound together by more tenacious cement. The white veins of quartz are also hard and resistant, creating ridges separating miniature valleys in the bedrock terrain.

Low tide on the winter beach often reveals beds of strikingly colored and patterned pebbles, sometimes mixed with shells and the larger rocks called cobble. The rocks were originally ripped from cliffs and shoreline boulders by the battering waves, were abraded into round or oval shapes and ground by the surf into progressively smaller sizes. They are all intermediate stages in a long process and eventually will be reduced to grains of sand. The sand particles, examined closely, reveal the same variety of color and pattern present in these rocks.

Jutting from the level sands of the beach below the cliffs at Fort Funston like the heads of some prehistoric monsters are occasional outcrops of strata belonging to the Merced formation, laid down at a time when the land was rising above the sea. The strata dip toward Lake Merced, for which they were named. These outcrops are usually covered by sand during the summer and are uncovered by the erosive power of the winter surf. The strata in the cliffs to the rear were deposited much later and belong to the Colma formation.

At Sand Dollar Beach, extending south of Fleishhacker Pool, you can often see the remains of these flat echinoderms that normally dwell on the sea bottom in deep water but are sometimes washed ashore. The sand dollar shell oddly bears a pattern like a five-petaled flower. Occasionally you may see the live animal within the shell, crawling slowly along the surface or burrowing into the wet beach, propelled by masses of soft spines on the underside.

A mass of serpentine, several shades of green interveined with quartz, is exposed on a pocket beach below the Presidio near the foot of a slide area. This is an intrusive rock which rose in a semiliquid state probably from the mantle of the earth, ten or twelve miles deep at this point, and flowed upward through fault zones in the crust. En route it may have picked up masses of metamorphic rock represented in boulders along this shoreline and in such sea stacks as Helmet Rock and Mile Rock. They are called "tectonic inclusions."

Part Two

THE TREES

Tree of Light

In San Francisco the sunlight reflects upward from the mirror of the bay to the hills; it gleams from the roaring white surf along the ocean boundary; it glares from the surface of fog banks rolling through the Golden Gate and over the coastal hills; and it reflects in subtle shades from the leaves of the eucalyptus trees in Golden Gate Park, in the Presidio, in Sutro Forest. In this relatively treeless community, the eucalyptus is the chief arboreal presence, and the effect of sunlight on its leaves is a distinctive quality of the city.

The eucalyptus light is not the bright metallic luster of the Lombardy poplars and the cottonwoods of the arid regions or the dazzling mirrorlike glitter of the quaking aspens in the high mountain passes; it is rather a muted scintillation like late afternoon sunlight on the blue-green waters of an ocean cove as seen through the filtering boughs of pines. This special quality of light is partly the result of the arrangement of the leaves. They are more widely spaced than those of the poplars and of many other trees whose leaves are often so dense that the observer can see only a wall of vegetation.

Look upward from a point near the base of a one-hundred-and-fifty-foot eucalyptus and you see terrace after terrace of foliage, each with its clusters of leaves shimmering with a different vibration as they are stirred by any slight movement of air. It is as if your eyes were moving upward from the base of a Gothic tower as the sunlight illuminated, one after another, successive rising arches and buttresses, spandrels and spires. In truth, each of these trees is a distinctive example of natural architecture, with its own variations of the principles of visual rhythm, balance, and proportion. No man-made towers display more variety and ingenuity of design.

It might be more appropriate, however, to compare the eucalyptus with contemporary rather than Gothic architecture. In keeping with the principles of modern architecture developed by Maybeck and Wright, the structural members—trunk and limbs—are largely visible and an essential part of the total visual effect. Unlike buildings and trees that hide their inner structure behind curtain walls or curtains of foliage, the eucalyptus has limbs that usually leave the trunk at an angle and sweep leaflessly upward in long arching lines before dividing into smaller leaf-bearing branches. The trunk and branches reach upward and outward in a flowing motion climaxed by spreading globular masses of lacy foliage, each shining with reflected sunlight.

This quality of light also is a result of the leaf attachment. The leaves of most trees extend stiffly outward from the branches, reaching for the sunlight, but in most species of eucalyptus the leaves—long, narrow, and curving like a scimitar—hang straight down. They move freely and separately in the breeze, suspended like Japanese wind chimes, resulting in a shimmering effect over the entire tree.

Visitors to the city are often surprised to learn that the eucalyptus is not a native of either this region or this hemisphere. It is difficult to imagine San Francisco—or California—without these trees, as the landscape appeared to the Forty-Niners, when there was not a single eucalyptus in the state. Where today the tall groves stand, the arriving Americans saw nothing but dunes, treeless hillsides, and open fields. During the early 1850s, with ships beginning to arrive regularly from Australia, it was inevitable that one of them would carry some of the aromatic pods of that continent's most abundant tree. Some may have been planted here as early as 1850, but the first large plantings on record were made about 1856 by nurseryman William C. Walker in his Golden Gate Nursery at Fourth and Folsom streets in San Francisco.

The city's major eucalyptus planters were William Hammond Hall,

8 3

Golden Gate Park's designer, who set out hundreds of them, along with Monterey pines and cypresses (many of the largest specimens at the park's east end, including the Panhandle, were set out by Hall in the early seventies); George Greene, Jr., who in the late seventies set out seedlings on his father's ranch, now Stern Grove; John McLaren, who, before he came to Golden Gate Park, planted many of the giant trees now growing along El Camino Real in Burlingame and San Mateo and continued Hall's plantings in the park; and Adolph Sutro, probably the champion planter of all, who set out hundreds of thousands of the trees in the 1890s, many of them still standing in thick groves on San Francisco's hills from Mount Sutro to Mount Davidson.

The Eucalyptus Rush

Since the days of the Mother Lode and the Comstock, California's economy had soared on a series of booms like a rocket with several stages, jet-propelled by a new explosion each time a previous impetus began to fizzle. In this boom-minded land it was perhaps inevitable that the eye of some energetic promoter would alight on the eucalyptus and he would have the same feeling James Marshall must have experienced when he first sighted the fateful gleam in the tailrace at Sutter's Mill in 1848.

The promoter's name has been lost to history, but the Eucalyptus Rush began half a century after the Gold Rush. The word got around quickly; beginning about 1904 the news began to spread that the eucalyptus was exactly the tree to put an end to the U.S. "hardwood famine." The eucalyptus was a timber tree in Australia, and a government booklet described its virtues as a possible source of hardwood. The State Forester glowingly predicted: "It would appear that this State will become within the next twenty years the base of hardwood supply and the home of hardwood manufacturing. The new industry will produce a greater wealth than oranges."

Promoters jumped in by the score. They bought up big tracts of land at prices around $15 an acre, set out eucalyptus seedlings that cost them only $5 a thousand and sold the land for $250 an acre, promising that within a decade the timber would be worth ten times that price. Modest proposals appeared in newspaper and magazine ads: "Put your surplus into eucalyptus and after ten years you can live on the income the rest of your life, and when you are gone your children and your children's children will perpetually reap the same."

Lured by the same promise of perennially flowing wealth that caused Americans by the millions to invest in gold mines, real estate, and oil wells, the eucalyptus boomers put cash on the line for title to a few acres planted to the magic new money tree. All over the State the seedlings were set out in forests that filled canyons and covered hillsides and bottomlands. The excitement lasted about eight years. Then somebody made the embarrassing discovery that there was more than one kind of eucalyptus. There were, in fact, in Australia a staggering six hundred species. And the principal kind imported here, the blue gum, was no good for timber, even in Australia.

Somebody might yet have imported the proper species and built up a thriving industry if it had not been for another disconcerting revelation. The trees used for timber in Australia were not ready for harvesting until they were several hundred years old. Few investors were sufficiently patient. So went the Eucalyptus Rush. And there went the fortunes of legions of the hopeful who had been certain that they had a sure thing.

Yet once-barren hills and valleys of California's lowlands are still clothed in thick forests—the overgrown remains of the big hardwood boom. And the trees have yielded scenic benefits quite apart from those expected by the planters. The huge groves planted by developer Frank Havens along the hills behind Berkeley and Oakland have proved valuable for another reason. They intercept the summer fogs that roll in from the ocean; the moisture condenses on their leaves and drips to the ground like steady rainfall, building up the water table. Rain gauges in Berkeley have measured seasonal fog-drip deposits of ten inches, equal to about half the normal annual rainfall for the area. Doubtless there is an equivalent effect in San Francisco's groves, particularly in thickly wooded Sutro Forest.

The fog-collecting capacity of the eucalyptus is partly a result of the same vertical foliage arrangement that gives the tree its reflective quality. The leaves, hanging loosely downward, present a barrier to the breeze-borne drops of fog vapor, which slide down the vertical leaf surfaces to the ground. Oddly, the juvenile leaves—on very young trees and new branches—do not have this quality; they are attached more rigidly, in conventional fashion. Then, at ages depending on the species and location, the leaves cease reaching upward for the sun and begin to hang down. Botanists puzzling over this peculiar change finally pieced together the explanation. In many species of both plants and animals, the individual when young passes quickly through the same stages of evolution that the species went through over a period of thousands of years. Every high-school biology student knows the formula: "Ontogeny recapitulates phylogeny." The history of the individual repeats the history of the species. The eucalyptus species went through some drastic changes. Evidently at some time in the distant past in its native Australia, the eucalyptus lived in a temperate climate where moderate sunlight was interrupted by intervals of overcast or stormy weather. The leaves, like those of most other vegetation, reached upward and outward to maximize their exposure to the light.

Slowly, owing to little-known causes, the Australian climate began to change, becoming increasingly sunny and arid. To cope with the new climate, the leaves slowly, over hundreds of generations, narrowed and began to hang vertically in order to turn the narrowest possible edge to the sun and avoid desiccation. In this odd habit of eucalyptus leaves, we read the record of immense climatic changes that probably covered large portions of the earth.

To see the results, look at some grove, such as Sutro Forest, where there has been little recent interference with natural processes. Here the prolific qualities of the eucalyptus are readily visible. The aromatic buds of the tree are thick under foot, and young seedlings, with their primordial upreaching leaves, sprout wherever there is sufficient light and moisture. Many a sapling, like an adolescent with both childlike and grown-up qualities, will bear juvenile and adult foliage simultaneously.

Silver Dollars and Shish Kebab

Striking changes took place in the eucalyptus over the eons as it spread across parts of barren Australia, where there was little competition from other trees, and adapted itself to innumerable varying climates and terrains. The result was the development of the six hundred species, most of which are unknown in California. But perhaps a hundred species have been introduced into this State. Of these, about two dozen are fairly common and supply endless variety to the city's eucalyptus landscapes.

There are two main groups—those that shed their bark and those that retain it the year around. The former are known to the unpoetic Australians simply as "gum trees," owing to the gummy substance that flows out of the wood to heal a wound. Because of its rapid growth (the record is seventy-five feet in ten years) the principal species of gum tree imported into California is one whose name comes from the color of juvenile foliage—blue gum, *Eucalyptus globulus.* If you can't identify a eucalyptus, call it a blue gum and chances are nine out of ten you'll be right. It is notable for its height— this is the true "skyscraper eucalyptus," commonly rising more than one hundred and fifty feet—and for aromatic pods that usually grow singly on the stem rather than in clusters, as do those of most other species.

The best-known blue gum in San Francisco is probably the spreading specimen in the middle of the Sixth Army Parade Ground in the Presidio, planted in 1876 in commemoration of the Nation's centennial. The tallest eucalyptus trees in North America are in the grove of blue gums near the West Gate of the University of California campus in Berkeley. They were planted in 1877, are about two hundred feet tall, and if transplanted in San Francisco's Union Square would tower over all the surrounding buildings. Near the campus grove, alongside the Life Sciences Building, is a superb example of *Eucalyptus viminalis,* known as manna gum or ribbon gum, from its habit of shedding bark in long dangling streamers. The underbark is often a striking cream color, and the species is sometimes called "white eucalyptus." There are several dozen of these in the Panhandle of Golden Gate Park, along with the more numerous blue gum. Occasionally the branches of the *viminalis* grows in graceful pendent fashion, resembling that of the weeping willow. There are several of this weeping kind in San Francisco along Park-Presidio Boulevard between Geary and the Presidio tunnel.

The most colorful species is *Eucalyptus ficifolia,* the trees that burst out across the city at various times of the year with explosions of red and orange, scarlet and crimson and cerise, along the streets and avenues, in backyards, in parks and gardens. Like other eucalyptus, the *ficifolia* is an unpredictable individualist. You may plant dozens of a particular species and find no two alike. The showy row of *ficifolia* along Bay Street at Fort Mason illustrates the variety of colors that turn up in a single planting.

The streets of San Francisco, which for a century have been treeless as the sand hills were, are being lined with eucalyptus and other species under the leadership of the city's street-tree chief, Brian Fewer, a tree planter in the best tradition of John McLaren and Adolph Sutro. Broad Van Ness Avenue, hitherto noted principally for its garish chrome-and-glass automobile emporiums, may well become the eucalyptus showplace of North America, as these trees do for the avenue what the chestnuts have done for the Champs Élysées. Eventually Van Ness will become a eucalyptus boulevard, displaying the tree in its innumerable variations.

Several species have odd-shaped leaves, unlike the typical long, narrow scythe-shaped leaves of the blue gum. The leaves of the *ficifolia* are shorter and broader than those of the blue gum. The silver-dollar eucalyptus (*Eucalyptus polyanthemos*) has dollar-sized silver-blue juvenile leaves which develop into a pointed oval shape. Three of these trees can be seen just west of the playground near the Nineteenth Avenue entrance to Golden Gate Park. The silver mountain gum (*Eucalyptus pulverulenta*) cannot be mistaken for any other species; its round silver-gray leaves surround the stems like an order of shish kebab on a skewer. Several young "shish kebab" trees grow on the south side of Golden Gate Park's Main Drive one hundred and fifty yards east of the Park-Presidio underpass.

The best place in the city to identify various kinds of eucalyptus is in Saint Francis Wood, the superbly landscaped residential district just west of Mount Davidson designed in 1912 by the late Frederick Law Olmsted, Jr. The trees here are trimmed and do not attain their full size and shape, but their trunks and foliage are easily identifiable. Along Saint Francis Boulevard and Santa Clara Avenue are visible the mottled and cream-colored trunks of the manna gum. On San Benito Way, Olmsted planted the silver-dollar tree and on San Leandro Way the red-flowered *ficifolia*. On Santa Ana Avenue are lanes of the broad-leaved desert gum and on Yerba Buena Avenue the weeping red gum, with pendulous boughs of lacy foliage, the most widely distributed species in Australia.

There are two particularly notable eucalyptus trees in Golden Gate Park. One is a spreading, triple-trunked blue gum opposite the old "Crystal Palace" Conservatory. It is reputed to be the oldest tree in the park, planted by some unknown settler in the 1860s, the decade before the park was laid out. The other is the hauntingly exotic *Eucalyptus cinerea* growing south of the Main Drive in a big meadow just beyond the museum area. Its leaves are a shimmering silver-blue, and in certain slants of sunlight it seems scarcely real, standing uncertainly at the far edge of the meadow against a wall of conventional foliage like a wraith of a mirage—the quintessence of the city's eucalyptic splendor.

The Raintree

In the confusing climate of the California coast, the first signs of spring come after the early rains in October or November, when the leaves of grass and the fragrant white flowers of that delightful weed the sweet alyssum begin to appear in the vacant lots and on the hillsides. But these signs are inevitably premature, for the weather becomes steadily colder, the storms sweep across the land, and the nights continue to lengthen toward the Christmas solstice. Then toward the end of January come the first genuine portents of great events in the plant world. Here and there buds begin to swell; a few plants, like the purple heather, tentatively venture some flowers; and among the leaves of the acacia trees there appear the first tentative indications of color—little more, at first, than a faint mist of pale yellow among the silver-green foliage.

Suddenly, at the beginning of February, as if with a fanfare of trumpets, the acacias blaze into a dazzle of yellow bloom and stand panoplied in all the brilliance of the season. The blossoms, rising like fountains of light and sweeping to the ground in billowing cascades, are the essence of spring. As tree after tree explodes into bloom, the light spreads from meadow to garden to hillside across Golden Gate Park and up the parkway joining it to the Presidio, across the old military post, through backyards in the Richmond and Sunset districts and around the bay from Sausalito to Saratoga. Everywhere the trees appear like yellow sunbursts against the rain-washed green of the young grasses and the other spring foliage.

Often the acacia blossoms have been compared to gold, but to this writer's eye they seem more like tangible masses of sunlight. The trees spring into blossom when they feel the touch of the added light that comes after the turn of the year, with the slow lengthening of the days as the sun begins its long northward climb, week by week, toward the summer solstice. And although the February weather may still be as cold as January and the storms may continue, even a few minutes of extra daylight is enough to set off the blooming of the acacias—the botanical equivalent of the ceremonial rejoicing of the ancients at the beginning of the sun's return.

The connection of the acacias with gold has a historical basis, however. The trees are not native to California; their seeds, like those of the eucalyptus, were first brought here from their native Australia by emigrants bound for the Gold Rush. Owing to their antecedents in the Southern Hemisphere, there is a common belief that the acacias' odd habit of blooming in winter is a hangover from the land of their origin, where the seasons are reversed. Actually, in their native habitat most of the acacias bloom in August—the Australian February. They adapted themselves to the California seasons soon after their arrival—although only a dozen or so of the hundreds of Australian varieties grow well here. These have taken up residence here so readily, however, that they seem indigenous.

Only three of the species growing in California have brilliant blossoms. First into bloom is the Bailey acacia (*Acacia baileyana*), which has fine feathery leaves; its flowers hang in large clusters of small yellow balls. There are some of these trees along the South Drive of Golden Gate Park near the Hall of Flowers. Following closely into bloom within a few days is the silver wattle (*Acacia decurrens*), with leaves and flowers very similar to those of the Bailey, although the trees grow almost twice as high, up to sixty feet. There are numbers of them along Golden Gate Park's Main Drive just west of the Conservatory.

The third of the showy species, blooming in March, is the Sydney golden wattle (*Acacia longifolia*). It is more of a bush, branching from the ground instead of from a trunk; its leaves (phyllodes) are not feathery but broad; and its blossoms form not in clusters of balls but on spikes an inch or two long. This species is not quite as spectacular in blossom as the other two, but it was planted by the thousands in Golden Gate Park by William Hammond Hall beginning in 1870, and later by John McLaren, because it grows lower and thus resists wind, needs less water, and has roots that help hold the sand. The black acacia (*Acacia melanoxylon*), with inconspicuous blossoms and dark green rather than silver-gray leaves, is often used as a street tree, although it has a picturesque but annoying habit of pushing sidewalks out of place. The flowering varieties have other disadvantages, well known to sufferers from hay fever.

In *Raintree County*, Ross Lockridge's novel about nineteenth-century Indiana, he tells of a legendary tree that grows at some unknown place on a remote island of the Grant Swamp in the center of the county, and whoever would glimpse the great tree, rising jetlike from the earth and raining yellow blossoms and pollen to the ground, would know the secret of life. I have always felt that the raintree must have been an acacia. Doubtless if there were but one of these trees in California, people would travel for hundreds of miles to see the spectacle.

Often the blossoms seem to have no smell at all, but occasionally a tree in full bloom gives off a sweet fragrance that is almost hypnotic; you are suddenly overwhelmed by memories of all the springtimes you have known, beginning long ago when the world was young and the sun was bright and the primal juices ran strong. Then this in truth becomes the raintree, and its secret is the secret of new life swelling in the spring—the secret of the lost Garden; and the return of the sun; and the fecund, flowering earth.

Australia's impressive botanical contributions to California have not been a one-way offering. California has contributed equally to the land Down Under, and residents of this State may feel as much at home there as Australians do when they encounter here their familiar gum tree. The Monterey pine, native only to the California coast and Guadeloupe Island in Baja California, has been planted by the thousands in Australia and produces that continent's principal softwood timber crop, covering half a million acres there and in New Zealand.

Like its companion tree of the central California shoreline, the Monterey cypress, it has been exported as well to the shores of the Mediterranean, to the South Pacific, to Africa and South America. Carefully pruned, it spreads with ornamental grace over the gardens of English manor houses, sometimes with giant branches trailing on the ground. It greets tree-conscious Californians with a touch of home in a dozen other countries with California-type climates from Spain to South Africa, from Kenya to Brazil. Industries based on Monterey pine turn out almost every kind of wood product from pulp and paper to plywood to lumber for construction. Here, however, its only product is beauty.

This pine has a venerable history. It was first sighted by Cabrillo when he sailed past the site of Monterey in 1542 and named the cape for the trees—

"Cabo de Pinos"—and the bay "Bahia de Pinos." Sixty years later Vizcaino anchored there, gazed in admiration at the pine forests covering the hills and speculated that they could furnish an ample supply of ships' masts for many generations. Two centuries later, after the Gold Rush, emigrating miners took seeds to New Zealand. In time, there and in Australia the Monterey pine became the prime softwood timber tree owing mainly to the lack of native pines there and to the tree's rapid growth. It is probably the fastest-growing pine on earth and under favorable conditions will shoot upward at a rate exceeding two feet a year for half a century or more.

The narrow range of the Monterey pine puzzled botanists for decades. Why does the tree grow naturally only in such a restricted area? The species is hardy and aggressive and by all rights should spread rapidly, but over the millenniums before it was carried around the world by man its natural range had become smaller rather than larger.

Besides the stand at Monterey, it grows indigenously only at two places in California: near Año Nuevo Point north of Santa Cruz and around the town of Cambria, south of San Simeon. But in the geologic past the tree grew along the California coast at least as far south as Carpinteria, near Santa Barbara, where fossil cones have been found in the tar pits. The ancient cones have also turned up north of the tree's present range, at Mussel Rock, on the ocean just south of San Francisco, and at Tomales Bay in Marin County. The fossils may offer a clue to the mystery: Mussel Rock is the point at which the San Andreas Fault goes out to sea, and Tomales Bay marks the line of the fault through Marin. It may be that some geologic unheavals connected with the fault—the longest on any continent—had a decisive effect on the species. The three coastal areas where these pines are native are all west of the fault. And these areas were evidently once part of Salinia, that ancient land mass that is believed to have once existed west of the present shoreline one hundred million years ago, a time when most of California was sea bottom and the waves broke on the foothills of the ancestral Sierra Nevada, one hundred and fifty miles to the east.

Over the eons Salinia, presumably the original home of the Monterey pine, eroded away into a series of islands (of which the Farallones are a remnant). Some of these islands became part of the newly risen mainland, and these are today the three botanic "islands" of Monterey pine along the coast. The tree comes down to us as a botanic vestige of an earlier epoch and a vanished landscape. There is even something primeval about its shape. Unlike the popular stereotype of the pointed pine tree, the Monterey often is eccentric, with a flat or rounded crown and branches taking off into space at all angles, as if it were a remnant of an era of freedom before the pines were regimented by evolution into the conventional shape.

Tree of the Continent's Edge

Even more numerous in San Francisco than the Monterey pine is its natural neighbor the Monterey cypress. The cypress too is a shoreline tree, has been planted throughout the world but grows indigenously only along the coast in restricted botanical "islands" that were once part of Salinia. In its natural habitat it is far rarer than the pine, however, and grows in even more grotesque shapes. All the millions of Monterey cypresses planted throughout the world are descendants of only two small groves in the vicinity of the headlands near the mouth of the Carmel River—Cypress Point on the Monterey Peninsula's Seventeen Mile Drive and Point Lobos a few miles south.

The cypresses are distinguished from the pines by their stubby scalelike leaves and small round cones. The pines have bigger curving cones, about four inches long, and finger-length needles. Even when planted, the cypresses, like the pines, grow only along temperate coastlines and are unknown in other parts of the United States, including Atlantic coast, where the winters are too cold for them. The cypresses are more restricted than the pines to the immediate coast however; they not only thrive on the damp winds, but they will not live far from the ocean. They owe their existence to the fact that they can grow in places where no other tree can survive.

At Point Lobos State Park you can see the reason. Away from the immediate shoreline they are unable to compete with the aggressive pines, which rise in thick groves behind the shore. But out on the very edge of the continent, on seacliffs where no pine—or any other tree—is hardy enough to live, battered by wind and stung by salt spray, the cypresses grip the granite with gnarled roots, built buttresses to the leeward, and lean away from the onslaughts of the ocean and the weather. The perennial sea winds sculpture them into fantastic contorted forms that seem lineal continuations of the ancient wave-worn rocks. They are natural material for legends, myths, and the Gothic imagination. Robert Louis Stevenson wrote during his stay in Monterey that their writhing shapes would make an appropriate setting for "a circle of the nether hell, as Dante pictured it." Donald Culross Peattie wrote that according to one myth these are the biblical Cedars of Lebanon, whose seeds were brought from the Holy Land by the Franciscan padres. Another tale has the seeds coming from the opposite direction, carried across the Pacific by Buddhist monks who came via the lost continent of Mu. The latter might be taken as a reference to the "lost continent" of Salinia, if it were not for the fact that Salinia disappeared long before the coming of man— even Buddhist monks.

The windswept San Francisco Peninsula was so similar to the windy, foggy Monterey coast that both pines and cypresses proved readily adaptable to this locale and were used by the founder of Golden Gate Park, William Hammond Hall, and later by John McLaren as pioneer trees to forest the dunes. In the sheltered eastern end of the park, including the Panhandle, both species grow to majestic heights. Many planted by Hall and McLaren in the park's early years are still standing as of this writing, but some of the largest would be destroyed by the proposed Panhandle Freeway.

The best-known single tree in San Francisco is a Monterey cypress rising to the height of a six-story building in front of McLaren Lodge in Golden Gate Park. This is the city's Christmas tree, a tower of multicolored lights during the holiday season. Probably few of the tens of thousands of people who drive by it are aware that this symmetrical monarch is the same species that grows in incredibly convoluted shapes on the headlands near the Carmel River.

Go west through Golden Gate Park and you can see both pines and cypresses undergo a sort of reverse evolution. The tall, well-shaped specimens growing in the east end of the park gradually give way to smaller, more wind-blown trees, and finally along the Great Highway at the ocean they are almost as dwarfed and wind-molded as in their native habitat. Near the ocean the conifers are pruned naturally by the wind into hanging terraces. Weak limbs are blown off, and the others trail out to the leeward, forming leafy strata separated vertically by natural wind tunnels.

Some of the city's most notable Monterey cypresses are growing at the

Fireman's Fund building, California and Presidio. They were planted nearly a century ago as part of the old Laurel Hill Cemetery, burial site of many of the city's pioneers, and were retained when the cemetery was moved and the company took over the hill in 1956. Two of the cypresses were apparently doomed by building expansion plans in 1965, but Fireman's Fund officials decided that the trees were of such value that they were justified in spending more than fifteen thousand dollars on special measures to save them.

Elsewhere in the city the cypresses are seen to best advantage along the northern shoreline at the Presidio and Lincoln Park. Standing not far apart in the Presidio are two contrasting groves. Near Julius Kahn playground, in a swale between the Arguello and Presidio avenue entrances, dozens of low cypresses join at the top to form an arboreal pavilion that seems darkly haunted even on the brightest days. The trees are scarcely more than fifteen to twenty feet high. On top of a hill to the west is an impressive grove of the same species rising to heights of sixty and seventy feet. The trunks in both groves range up to two and three feet in diameter, indicating that they are roughly the same age and were evidently planted shortly after the turn of the century.

Ordinarily it might be assumed that the smaller trees were more exposed to the winds, but in this case the lower trees are in a more protected area. The reason for their dwarf size is not hard to find, however. Directly across the Presidio wall are the venerable mansions of Presidio Heights, looking out over the top of the grove to the bay. Every two years the residents receive permission to have the trees topped, at their expense, to preserve their view.

Adolph Sutro originally planted both Monterey cypresses and pines in large numbers on Mount Sutro, but the more aggressive blue-gum eucalyptus have taken over in the decades since, and the conifers in Sutro Forest are now relatively rare, although a few tall ones grow in advantageous locations. Some of the largest and best-formed cypresses grow on the golf courses at the Presidio and Lincoln Park, where they line the fairways and provide the best kind of windbreaks in this breezy area. The trees can be seen in conditions closest to their native habitat on the cliffs of the Golden Gate below Lincoln Park. There they grow in eloquent wind-hewn shapes or cluster to form thick low groves with openings like tunnels where you can wander endlessly down winding corridors or into frustrating dead ends, half expecting to see a wizened gnome appear around the next bend of the mystic maze. And who knows? He might introduce himself as a resident of Salinia.

Yerba Buena

One of the prevalent myths concerning early-day San Francisco is the belief that its original sand hills were as barren as the dunes of the Sahara. It is true that Father Font, chaplain of the Anza expedition which founded San Francisco in 1776, noted while camped at Mountain Lake that "there is not a tree on all these hills." And ninety years later Frederick Law Olmsted, Sr., father of American landscape architecture, remarked in his plan for a park system for the city that the continual winds prevented the growth of "so much as a single full-sized tree."

Yet this peninsula tip was rich in native plant life and even after a century of development still has what botanist John Thomas Howell calls "one of the outstanding local floras of California." Font himself was impressed with the fertility of the soil, and wrote that "this place and its vicinity has abundant pasturage, plenty of firewood, and fine water, all good advantages for establishing here the presidio or fort which is planned." The peninsula had an abundance of wildlife: "The soldiers chased some deer, of which we saw many today . . . We also found antlers of the large elk." And its hills were carpeted in that spring of 1776 with flowers: ". . . Here near the lake there are yerba buena and so many lilies that I had them almost inside my tent."

The yerba buena ("good herb") was a creeper with an aromatic mint flavor that the Spaniards liked to use for tea. It was supposed to cure various ailments. It grew so prolifically in damp sheltered areas that a cove near the peninsula's northeastern corner was named for it. By 1792 an island off the cove and later the village at the cove were given the name of the plant. The village became San Francisco; the cove was filled in; and only the island retains the name. On this windy peninsula the sheltered, well-watered areas where the yerba buena grew were the first to be claimed for building sites, and there is now no yerba buena growing wild in the city, although its heady scent can be detected in the Garden of Fragrance for the Blind at Strybing Arboretum in Golden Gate Park.

No one knows what type of "lily" Padre Font found almost inside his tent at Mountain Lake, but it is possible he was mistakenly referring to the California poppy which still grows by the millions across the hillsides in spring. The explorers called it "copa de oro," cup of gold, but it received its unpronounceable official name from a Frenchman. His name was Adelbert von Chamisso; he arrived here in 1816 on the Russian ship *Rurick*, and he explored these hills with all the excitement of an Adam naming the new plants in a botanical Eden. Doubtless he first sighted what was to become the California state flower when the crew of the *Rurick* put ashore at the Presidio, and he named it *Eschscholzia californica* for his friend, Johann Friedrich Eschscholtz, the ship's doctor.

Eschscholtz responded in a gesture of gallantry by giving Chamisso's name to the blue beach lupine, *Lupinus chamissonis*, that grew abundantly in the same area. In combination with the *Eschscholzia californica*, the blue lupine spreads across the coastal hills and valleys the state colors, blue and gold. Its larger relative, the yellow beach lupine (*Lupinus arboreus*) was discovered even earlier by the English botanist Archibald Menzies, who was here with Vancouver in 1792 and found it growing in head-high stalks across the dunes on the oceanward side of the peninsula—as it does today in the few sandy areas not yet built upon, particularly around Point Lobos and Land's End, in the Presidio, in Golden Gate Heights. The seeds remain in the pods often through the winter and rattle in the wind like a child's toy.

Chamisso enthusiastically collected other plants that grew in abundance and can still be seen over the sand and clay soils, such as the fragrant-leaved sagebrush (*Artemisia*) and the coyote brush (*Baccharis*), sometimes called "fuzzy-wuzzy" owing to its fluffy windblown seeds that give a blond hue to the slopes in the fall. His friend Eschscholtz was a scarcely less assiduous collector, and identified the coffee berry (*Rhamnus californica*), which still grows in thickets on hills and bluffs, and the blue blossom or wild lilac (*Ceanothus thyrsiflorus*), which covered the city's western hills with dazzling blues in the spring but now is found only occasionally in such places as the cliffs west of the Golden Gate Bridge and the brushy hills in the Presidio.

"Woods for Murderers"

Here and there in the historical records are hints that some mysterious conifer once grew naturally on this peninsula tip before the coming of civilization. Menzies in 1792 wrote about tufts of unidentified trees on the ridges above Mission Dolores; they could conceivably have been conifers, since broad-leafed trees seldom grow on windy summits. Later visitors reported an unknown conifer growing on Lone Mountain. What it might have been is anybody's guess. It is conceivable that these were Monterey pines, as fossil cones of that tree have been found in this region. Another clue is intriguing. Workmen excavating for buildings at the University of California Medical Center on Mount Sutro reported finding remains of redwoods.

Redwoods, which require large quantities of water and a sheltered environment, could scarcely have been growing on the ridge tops, but conceivably the trees might have taken root in canyons or on the lee sides of hills. San Francisco is the only county along six hundred miles of California coastline from San Luis Obispo to the Oregon border where redwoods do not seem to grow naturally, owing mainly to the lack of shelter from the perennial sea winds. But redwoods planted by John McLaren in Golden Gate Park have grown to substantial sizes, and at least one reaches a diameter of about four feet. It seems to be directly in the path of the proposed freeway, however.

Padre Font had occasion, after a few days exploration, to revise his initial impression as to the absence of trees. He reported no conifers, but there were —and still are—small willows along Lobos Creek and other streams; there were oaks and laurels in the shallow canyons at the base of what is now Pacific Heights and buckeyes on the hills; there were fairly thick groves of scrub oaks on sheltered slopes of Russian and Nob hills and along a low ridge near the northeast corner of what is now Golden Gate Park.

The laurels (*Umbellularia californica*), which also grew along the bay shore for a considerable distance east of Fort Point, were collected and described by Menzies in 1792, and have since acquired several names; they are known as bay trees, and in Oregon as pepperwood or myrtle. Unfortunately, this species, which has pungently aromatic leaves, succumbed to civilization in San Francisco, although laurels are found in abundance in the Tamalpais region just north of the Golden Gate.

The oaks almost met the same fate, but a few still grow on hillsides around Lake Merced, at Lobos Creek, and in the Presidio and in Golden Gate Park. These are the coast live oak (*Quercus agrifolia*), called "encina" by the Spaniards in distinction to "roble," the deciduous oak growing farther inland. Both names are used as place names throughout California. Only one sizable grove still exists here in its natural habitat; it is in Golden Gate

Park on Conservatory Ridge and in the nearby swales along the northeastern edge of the park, an area also threatened by the proposed freeway. Here (as of 1967) you can walk through a typical California live-oak woodland, where the old trees form fascinating hyperbolic shapes. Stevenson exercised his morbid imagination on these trees, too, during his sojourn at Monterey, and described their twisted forms as "woods for murderers to crawl among."

The live oaks seldom grow vertically. Their trunks (they may have two or three) usually extend themselves horizontally after getting a few feet off the ground, twisting and turning and very often coming down again to ground level, making them irresistible to youngsters fond of emulating our arboreal ancestors. The live-oak leaves do not have the lobes of the deciduous oak leaves but are simple oval shapes, have small spines along the edges and when turned upside down are sufficiently concave to hold water.

These are the trees pictured in a thousand paintings and postcards of "typical" California hillside scenes, their gnarled contorted trunks accentuated by a background of grasses that are gold in summer and fall, green in winter and spring, with the blue of lupine and the yellow of poppies spread across rolling hillsides. Walking through the grove in the park, the old-time Californian can picture the open hills of his youth, before the bulldozers came, and remember Sunday afternoon picnics on a hundred pastoral slopes of the Coast Range foothills overlooking fertile valleys yet unsubdivided. He can remember the feel of the gnarled gray bark on his hands as he hoisted himself along the trunks, the crackle of the stiff leaves between his fingers and the good oak smell of the foliage and of the long, pointed acorns.

Nearly a century ago William Hammond Hall, the park's founder, recognized the value of these trees, mere scrubs when he laid out the park in the 1870s, and cultivated them until they grew into sizable specimens. After the earthquake and fire of 1906, when thousands of displaced people were camped in the park, many of the live oaks were stripped for firewood, but they recovered and have again attained a respectable size. Increasing numbers of live oaks across the California countryside are destroyed for subdivisions or perish because of a falling water table as wells suck out the water from beneath them, and it is to be hoped that Golden Gate Park's live-oak grove will be cherished as the only native woods in the city and as representative of a race that once was spread for thousands of square miles across the hills and valleys of the California coast.

99

There are few more hardy trees in the San Francisco climate than the blue-gum eucalyptus. A single tree, LEFT, may bear hundreds of thousands of aromatic seed pods (believed to be medicinally beneficial), scattering them on the wind into such unlikely places as a crevice between big rocks, where a handful of soil may be enough to nourish the seeds. Sometimes so many of the seeds germinate that the trees grow a few inches apart, as in parts of neglected Sutro Forest, and saplings grow as tightly as a canebrake, denying each other the light and soil they need to grow into such magnificent specimens as those around Chain of Lakes, BELOW, in Golden Gate Park.

The varied forms of the eucalyptus are particularly visible in the Panhandle of Golden Gate Park, where trees planted nearly a century ago tower over the broad lawns and the Victorian houses along the adjoining streets.

The bark of the manna gum, peeling in long strips to reveal the white underbark, exhibits striking patterns and textures that are variously smooth or rough, wavy or zigzagged, mottled or marbled.

Although the eucalyptus plantations of San Francisco are dominated by the ubiquitous blue gum, among the hundreds of eucalyptus species are such distinctive types as the red-flowering eucalyptus, represented by the symmetrical specimen, LEFT, bearing brilliant blossoms in the middle of Van Ness Avenue near the splendid Renaissance dome of City Hall. BELOW, in Golden Gate Park the sun backlights the leaves of a young silver-dollar eucalyptus and reflects from the equally silvery leaves of the "shish-kebab" eucalyptus, which appear to be impaled on a skewer.

The word eucalyptus is from the Greek prefix *eu*, meaning "good" or "well," and *kalyptos*, which means "covered." The seed pod on the eucalyptus is "well covered" by a tightly fitting lid which falls off when the pod is ripe and the seeds are ready to be distributed. The lids, shaped like shallow thimbles, can be found on the ground beneath the trees, along with the aromatic pods. On the blue gum shown here, the covered pods, which bear the flowers, are white at first, but after the blossoms fall, the pods turn brown as they ripen. The blossoms appear to be small explosions of white against the admirable patterns of the scimitar-shaped leaves.

The stately Monterey cypress can be
seen in front of McLaren Lodge in
Golden Gate Park, where it performs
holiday duty as the city's lighted Christmas tree, and behind Adolph Sutro's
statuary at Sutro Heights, mingling with
the tall pines.

Scarcely recognizable as the same species are the cypresses in the groves that form a dark pavilion in the Presidio and stretch before the wind in contorted streamlined shapes along the cliffs of the Golden Gate.

The long-leaved Monterey pine grows in innumerable shapes and forms but always has an air of majesty and grace and is singularly appropriate to its environment, whether it rises above Golden Gate Park's exquisitely anachronistic Victorian Conservatory, leans to the leeward on a clifftop high above the fog flowing through the Golden Gate, or reflects the dignity of a venerable Queen Anne house on the Panhandle.

In February the acacias burst out in masses of yellow bloom on Telegraph Hill over the bay and at such other locations as Edgewood, that embowered street of big old houses hidden high on the eastern slope of Mount Sutro. The plum blossoms of Edgewood simultaneously turn that neighborhood into a dazzle of pink and white.

The mesembryanthemum is a succulent that creeps across the ground in the dune areas of Golden Gate Heights and elsewhere. The variety pictured is the common mesembryanthemum or "Hottentot fig," a reference to the fruit borne by the plant. In spring and summer it has showy blossoms ranging from yellow to pink. It is a native of South Africa, often planted here on dunes and road cuts to prevent erosion. Another species of mesembryanthemum is commonly called "ice plant." Only one of the several species of mesembryanthemum is native to this region; it has shorter leaves and deep mauve flowers and can be seen on the dunes at Bakers Beach.

"Spring" in San Francisco may range over a period of eight months, beginning in October or November when the first rains bring the fragrant sweet alyssum, ABOVE, which is not a native but grows wild on vacant lots, dunes, and hillsides. The Spanish broom, RIGHT, comes out in bright yellow by March.

A little later you may encounter along the clifftops of the Golden Gate, ABOVE, the candlelike heads of hare's-tail grass. In May and June the indigenous yellow lupine, RIGHT, covers such sandy slopes as this one at the Presidio.

The agave or "century plant" is an arid-land cactus that oddly seems to thrive in foggy windy areas, as does this one on Russian Hill. Its wicked swordlike leaves grow for many years before sending up their blossoms on the end of a trunk that may rise fifteen feet or more. The notion that the plants bloom only once in a hundred years, however, is strictly mythological.

Among the city's most venerable trees are these oriental-shaped Monterey cypresses at the Fireman's Fund building, California and Presidio streets, and the blue-gum eucalyptus on the parade ground at the Presidio. The cypresses (one behind the other), remnants of the vanished Laurel Hill Cemetery, are probably a hundred years old, and Fireman's Fund spent thousands of dollars in special measures to preserve the prized specimens when the building was expanded.

The magnificent eucalyptus was planted by Angelo Bareta, post trader, in 1876 to commemorate the nation's centennial. It has surprisingly survived despite the extension of the pavement almost up to the trunk, depriving its roots of water, and would possibly be even larger if it were well cared for. Proper nurture would make more likely its survival to the nation's bicentennial and beyond.

113

Wander through almost any section of the city and if you keep a sharp eye out you will continually spot surprising scenes in the plant world, such as the overgrown tangles of white marguerites and other plants among century-old houses on the steep eastern

slope of Telegraph Hill . . . or the tracery of flowering fruit blossoms against the geometrical lines of a Victorian house in the Richmond district.

Offbeat tree shapes are found in this wind-twisted Norfolk Island pine, ABOVE LEFT, on lower Twin Peaks; in the elephantine branch of this *Sequoia gigantea*, ABOVE RIGHT, at the Panhandle's eastern end; in the writhing limbs of these sycamores and elms, BELOW, at Golden Gate Park's Music Concourse, where crowds sit in the winter sunshine to hear a band concert. These trees are dwarfed by pruning to maintain the view over the top of the sunken Concourse.

Along the northeastern edge of Golden Gate Park is a woodland of coast live oaks representing San Francisco's principal native tree. The live oaks' habit of leaning almost horizontally results in weird contorted shapes resembling animals or humans and makes them irresistibly attractive to young tree-climbers. This grove, nurtured by William Hammond Hall a century ago, is threatened by a proposed freeway.

California Street, descending to Polk Gulch and rising up Nob Hill, is lined by sycamores set out as part of a plan to turn the city's traditionally barren streets into shaded arboreal avenues. The tree across the street on the left is a Norfolk Island pine.

Part Three

THE PARKS

The Vision of Frederick Law Olmsted

The truth should be faced, heretical though it may be: man-made San Francisco is an ugly city. With the exception of a very few well-designed buildings, most of the works of man here are unworthy of the site. It is nature that gives the city its distinction—the hills, the climate, the surrounding waters. Without them San Francisco would be almost indistinguishable from a hundred other cities. Yet there are at least three man-made features of the city commensurate with the magnificence of the natural setting. They are the Golden Gate Bridge, the Bay Bridge, and Golden Gate Park.

This park is the city's greatest work of art. Like many another work of art, it is the result of man's creative use of materials provided by nature. Perhaps nowhere else on earth has land with so little promise been so thoroughly transformed by the art of landscape design. The thousand acres of Golden Gate Park are windows through which we may look out of the man-made hive into the larger natural world beyond. We can, so to speak, step through the windows, leave behind the concrete and asphalt and accelerating pressures of urban life, and find in the park's woods and meadows, its groves and dells, it lakes and streams, its birds and wildlife, the kind of refreshment and renewal essential to sanity in this frenetic era.

The park came into being through a fortuitous set of circumstances that could scarcely have coincided at any other time in history. The decade of the

1860s was a propitious time for the beginning of a city park system. The Gold Rush had brought to San Francisco not merely untutored frontiersmen but men of learning from the East Coast and Europe, men of talent and imagination fascinated by the prospect of a new and promising center of civilization here on the shores of the Pacific. At the same time the Gold Rush and the booms that followed it had developed a class of men of wealth who became aware of the need for civic amenities. Frontier San Francisco was crude, ugly, and totally without the cultural marks of urban distinction— notable civic buildings, boulevards, museums, parks.

Simultaneously, in the nation's large cities, there was an incipient movement to preserve and develop large natural areas within urban boundaries. The most outstanding example was New York's Central Park, which was being designed and developed by Frederick Law Olmsted, Sr. And there was a further fortunate coincidence: the courts in the mid-1860s were confirming San Francisco's title to the "Outside Lands"—the sand dunes constituting what is now the western part of the city—and such leading citizens as millionaire Samuel Brannan (the man who started the Gold Rush) believed that a large part of the new area should be devoted to a public park. They secured the services of Olmsted, who had been living temporarily in California developing the former Frémont ranch in the Sierra foothills and was intermittently in the Bay Area designing the University of California campus in Berkeley. Olmsted's foresight extended in many directions. It was during this California stay that he was one of the prime movers in obtaining Federal action to set aside Yosemite Valley for park purposes—the first step toward the concept of a national park system.

For San Francisco, Olmsted recommended a park system including a "sea gate" and parade ground at the foot of Van Ness Avenue, a sunken parkway along Van Ness, other parkways throughout the city, and a hundred-and-twenty-acre park in the lee of Buena Vista Hill. His specific suggestions were not followed (although Aquatic Park was eventually established at the foot of Van Ness), but he helped kindle enthusiasm for a major park. He urged "a pleasure ground second to none in the world," planned for the "convenience not merely of the present population, or even of their immediate successors, but of many millions of people."

Mayor Frank McCoppin appointed a "Committee on Outside Lands," to recommend a site for such a park. Several areas were considered, including

119

the Presidio, for its spectacular location on the Golden Gate, and the Mission district, for its sheltered position in the lee of Twin Peaks. The area that was finally chosen, however, apparently had little to recommend it except for its vast size—more than a thousand acres—and the fact that the land could be acquired cheaply. It was a long half-mile-wide strip running from the geographical center of the city to the ocean, consisting principally of sand dunes.

The Faith of William Hammond Hall

The selection of William Hammond Hall to begin the job of creating Golden Gate Park in 1870 was one of those lucky accidents that change the course of history. He was selected mainly because he was the only person intimately familiar with the terrain. As a young engineer during the 1860s he had been making geographical maps of the desolate western areas of the city for the Army Engineers, who oddly enough were concerned with getting information that would be useful in fortifying San Francisco against possible attack by the British. (There had been fears in Washington during the Civil War that Britain might intervene on the side of the Confederacy.)

After finishing a survey of the park area for the city in 1870, Hall was placed in charge of the entire project. He confronted a dismal prospect—a sea of dunes, a few acres of clay and rock at the eastern end of the area, and a hundred-foot hill about one third of the way to the ocean, where some wild strawberries had taken root. Because it was the only area of vegetation in a sea of sand, what is now Strawberry Hill was originally known as "The Island." (By a curious coincidence it literally was turned into an island in later years when Stow Lake was constructed entirely around it.)

While making his survey, Hall developed a comprehensive plan for a park whose main outlines are those of the park today. Doubtless he had studied Olmsted's plan for Central Park, as there are remarkable similarities between the two designs. At that time, however, the proposal that this "desert" should or could be turned into a park was condemned as ridiculous by newspapers, magazines, horticultural experts, and a good many leading citizens and taxpayers. The dunes were absolutely "unsusceptible to cultivation," one newspaper said. "No amount of labor or money will serve to make anything of them . . ."

"It was generally believed and repeatedly urged by a good portion of the local press," Hall wrote later, in 1886, "that any attempt to build and maintain a park on the dry sands and brush-covered hillocks which composed the site, would prove a costly failure. Powerful and winning pens, whose ink has within the past decade flowed in gratulation at the results attained and to be expected in Golden Gate Park, were within the ten years before busily engaged in denouncing the selection of the place for the purpose—declaring that no park could be built there, and no verdure maintained, at any cost which the city could afford."

Hall knew better. He had camped in the dunes and tramped over nearly every foot of them all the way to the ocean. He knew that in certain protected areas, such as the lee of Strawberry Hill, wild plants had managed to find a foothold. He had learned that they were able to find nourishment in the sand by sending out incredibly long roots. Wild lupine that grew only two or three feet in height sent down roots twenty feet into the sand. He discovered a sand willow with roots one hundred and twenty-five feet long. To most observers the dunes seemed completely waterless, but Hall dug below the dry surface and found moisture at a depth of less than a foot. The dry layer of sand on the surface served as a mulch to protect the moist layers from the desiccating sun and wind. He observed that even when quantities of new sand were blown over the top of the dry surface layer, capillary attraction raised the water level to within a foot of the new surface.

Hall found, too, that on cloudy days he was able to lie down comfortably on the warm sand at times when other soils were cold. This experience indicated that the sand was able to store heat absorbed from the sun. Another advantage of sand was that rain water did not run off but sank in deeply and was retained in the moist lower layers. For all these reasons Hall found that in many ways sand provided better conditions for plants than other types of soil. It would require more fertilizer, but ample quantities of manure were available from the sweepings of the stables.

First, some "pioneer" plant would have to be sowed to hold the sand in order that trees could take root and the area could be forested. The logical plant for the job was the native lupine. But Hall faced a dilemma. How could he sow lupine in the dunes—where the movement of sand was obviously too great for them to grow naturally? With the help of San Francisco historian Hubert Howe Bancroft, Hall obtained foreign publications on dune reclamation and learned that the common method in Europe was to scatter loose

121

brush over the soil to protect the first seedlings until they were able to gain a foothold. In the sand hills of San Francisco, however, there was not enough brush available to cover the vast acreage of the park.

The solution was supplied by a fastidious horse. On one occasion when Hall was camped in the dunes near one of the natural ponds which have since been made into the Chain of Lakes, his horse accidentally upset the pail of barley and water from which the animal had been feeding. Hall impatiently scooped up some of the barley and put it back into the pail, but the horse disdained the sandy meal. Hall disgustedly threw out the entire contents of the pail. A light rain fell soon afterward, and a day or two later he was amazed to find the discarded barley sending up green sprouts across the sand. Within ten days the patch was covered with a vigorous growth of the grain. Hall was jubilant. He could sow barley, a seasonal plant, to hold the sand until the perennial lupine could grow under its protection and gain a foothold. His first major problem had been solved. Unfortunately, the name of the horse responsible for the historic discovery was not recorded for posterity.

In more exposed areas where the sand drifted too fast for even the barley to take root, Hall resorted to a method widely used in Europe; he sowed beach grasses of the kind that continue to grow as the sand covers them until the dunes reached a height over which the sand will no longer blow. In the sands held by the grasses and lupine he planted throughout the area thousands of young trees of hardy varieties—Monterey pine and cypress, eucalyptus and acacia. Many of today's biggest trees in the park, particularly those in the Panhandle and around the eastern end, were set out by Hall in the six years after 1870.

Hall's accomplishments seemed miraculous. The most bitter critics of a park in the sand wastes were won over. By 1876 nearly all of the thousand acres had been planted with trees, and the park was replacing Woodward's Gardens (a kind of early-day Disneyland in the Mission district) as San Francisco's chief recreation area. A carriage ride to the park on a Sunday afternoon was standard entertainment. Newspapers that had originally denounced the attempt praised the park's roads, its picnic grounds, its young groves. One paper that had been particularly critical gave Hall extravagant praise: "A finer drive than this one is not to be found on the continent."

Frederick Law Olmsted, Sr., who had kept in touch with Hall and had given advice and encouragement, had superlative praise for the achievement: "No more difficult problem has probably ever been presented in our profession," he wrote, "than that involved in the San Francisco park undertaking . . . It is much greater than that which we met in Central Park or in any other work . . . I cannot too strongly express my admiration . . . There is no like enterprise anywhere else which . . . has been conducted with equal foresight, ingenuity, and economy."

The Park and the Politicians

William Hammond Hall's day of glory was short-lived. Powerful political interests were after his scalp. Throughout his term as park chief the young engineer was almost as busy fighting politicians and promoters as he was combating the wind and sand that buried his plantings. One of his first jobs was to evict squatters from the newly acquired park lands, and he was as tough with them as he was with the politicians later. On one occasion in 1871 he ordered his men to padlock a squatter cabin on Buena Vista Peak while the inhabitants were absent. (The hill was originally intended to be part of Golden Gate Park but the intervening property could not be acquired by the city, and it became a separate park.) Hall described the incident with the squatters or "roughs" in later years: "I secreted several armed men in the bushes on the hillside above the cabin and myself stayed by to see that no one shirked. The roughs came with a heavy timber and started to batter down the cabin door. We fired several rounds of shots over the cabin roof. The roughs returned the fire but never came back."

Hall's steely methods with the squatters were less successful with the politicians. He had the misfortune to live in an era of acute municipal corruption that was to be climaxed by the notorious régime of San Francisco Boss Abe Ruef. As the city expanded toward the ocean, there were some munificent profits to be made—legally and illegally—in contracts for grading and paving the new streets. The construction of the City Hall was so riddled with graft that it was one of the few buildings to be shaken down in the earthquake of 1906. (Most of the damage elsewhere was in the fire that followed.) When the newspapers attacked the graft connected with the Street Department and the City Hall, then under construction, and simultaneously praised Hall and the Park Commission as models of honesty and efficiency, the "Street Gang" and the "City Hall Gang" zeroed in on Hall for making them look so bad by comparison.

In his first few years, however, Hall was in an almost impregnable position. One of his best friends was the most powerful man in San Francisco—William Chapman Ralston, Comstock Lode millionaire, chief of the Bank of California, and builder of the original Palace Hotel. Driving his team into the city from his home in Belmont, following El Camino Real and the route of Nineteenth Avenue, Ralston would frequently stop in the park for a chat with his young friend. Together the two planned an ambitious project to plant and landscape the entire western part of the city along the lines of Golden Gate Park. If the idea had materialized, the present-day Sunset and Richmond districts might well have come to resemble the wooded community of Carmel. Ralston was persuading his friends who owned most of the property in the area when tragedy struck. The Bank of California collapsed and the banker, who was accustomed to taking a daily swim in the bay at North Beach, drowned shortly afterward.

Hall's enemies then began to close in. Their attack anticipated a strategy to be widely used in our own era. They arranged for the park chief to be "investigated" by a committee of the Legislature, which then controlled the park. The impartiality of the proceedings may be judged by the fact that the chief investigator was a former park employee who some years earlier had been fired by Hall for dishonesty. Conveniently for the City Hall Gang, Hall had made other enemies as well. One faction, backed for obvious reasons by grading contractors, insisted that the dunes in the park area should be leveled and the entire area as formally landscaped as the Garden of Versailles. On the other side were commercial nurserymen, some of them miffed at Hall for failing to patronize them, who were opposed to the slightest tampering with the natural contours. They were particularly irate when he cut the park's Main Drive through a ridge between the eastern park entrance and the valley where the glassy old Conservatory now stands, using the debris to fill a series of "frog ponds" and create the long meadow just inside the eastern gate.

The sharpest weapon in the hands of Hall's enemies was the charge that he was chopping down trees that he had admittedly planted just a few years earlier—evidence, his opponents trumpeted, of mismanagement, inefficiency, and shameful waste of the taxpayers' money. One editorial wailed: "It is a sacrilege to cut down a well-grown tree!" Actually, Hall had followed the regular horticultural practice of planting young trees in thickets for mutual protection from the wind, then thinning them out when they were big enough to stand on their own. Far from being wasteful, Hall was using the cut trees to help build up the "dike" along the ocean to diminish the sand drift. But the park's founder was a man who disdained to take notice of his detractors by replying to their accusations. All of Hall's opponents had their innings during the investigation. Before it was over, they had steamrollered through the Legislature a bill slicing his park budget to almost zero. Hall's response was characteristically uncompromising. He condemned the budget cut as a measure to "cripple the park," pronounced a curse on his enemies, and stalked out of the job.

During what Hall called the Dark Decade, 1876–1886, Golden Gate Park struggled along with scanty funds under several successive superintendents. Many of Hall's young trees were buried in sand or died for lack of care. Olmsted, alarmed at what was happening to so promising a project, wrote an urgent letter to the city fathers warning that a continual change of managements could lead to the park's "ruination." Partly as a result of Olmsted's warning and partly owing to a change in the political situation, Hall was called back in 1886 to save the park. By that time he had become California's first State Engineer and could not give the park his full time, but he agreed to train a new superintendent to work under him.

His choice for the job was a young Scottish gardener named John McLaren, who had done outstanding work landscaping private estates down the peninsula (and whose tall eucalyptus trees still stand along El Camino Real and elsewhere in the vicinity). Meanwhile, Hall had begun thinning out his original plantings, which during the Dark Decade had been "allowed to stand much too thickly grown," he reported, "until they were . . . ruined for form and vigor." Once again came the chorus of critics with the theme: "Woodsman, spare that tree"—the title of a newspaper editorial. Hall weathered the storm this time, however, only to face a blow from another direction.

As State Engineer he had clashed frequently with the political machine of the Southern Pacific Railroad (which then dominated California) and with the S.P.'s man in Sacramento, W. W. Stow. When Stow was appointed park commissioner in 1889, Hall exploded, claiming that Stow wanted to turn the park into a "Coney Island." Once again the uncompromising engineer had no alternative but to resign, leaving McLaren in charge.

Hall continued as State Engineer, guided the development of many of the early irrigation projects that turned California's drylands into fertile valleys, and became a world authority on irrigation engineering. He was called to South Africa by empire builder Cecil Rhodes to develop an irrigation system for Rhodesia and later did similar work for the Tsar in Russia and for several other countries. But for forty-five years after leaving Golden Gate Park, until his death in 1934, Hall kept a proprietary eye on the park, smoldering with rage every time it was invaded by what he regarded as Coney Island attractions—fairs, museums, race tracks, and stadiums. As might be expected, his park philosophy was a stern and uncompromising devotion to a single principle. The purpose of a "city woodland park," he maintained, was to provide an area of nature in urban surroundings, a place of quiet repose and a retreat from the tense, noisy atmosphere of a large city. Big buildings, sports arenas, and other urban features should be kept out as violations of the park's purposes.

During his own period of control he had repulsed what he regarded as attacks on the park's integrity as a natural refuge, including the proposal of Adolph Sutro to build a Parisian boulevard across the park, and what he called a "damnable scheme"—backed by powerful Spring Valley Water Company—to turn most of the eastern end of the park into a reservoir. His opposition was not diminished by the fact that an executive of the Spring Valley Water Company was one of his bosses as a member of the Park Commission. He felt that later "intrusions" were inexcusable and was particularly scornful toward Stow's policy of inducing wealthy citizens to donate features to the park to be named after themselves. Sweeney's Observatory on Strawberry Hill (destroyed in 1906) was a case in point. And he opposed the plan to hold in the park the Midwinter Fair of 1894, which resulted in the present music concourse and museum area. "The value of a park," Hall said, "consists of its being a park, and not a catch-all for almost anything which misguided people may wish upon it."

He reserved his most caustic criticism for the feature of the park planned by and named after his political foe—an artificial lake wrapped around the side of a hill, he said, like "a shoestring tied around a watermelon." Both Stow Lake and Huntington Falls tumbling into it from the open face of Strawberry Hill were, he felt, freaks and offenses to nature and the art of landscaping. But even more flagrant violations of his "woodland park" were

1 2 6

to come—Kezar Stadium, for example, and a six-lane expressway bisecting the park, connecting Nineteenth Avenue and Park-Presidio Boulevard. Hall's original design called for four drives to carry traffic across the park, sunken below ground level, bridged by pedestrian walks and screened by foliage, following Olmsted's example in Central Park. Had this plan been followed, the perennial traffic threats to the park would have been avoided.

Possibly there are few people today who would take the sternly uncompromising stand of William Hammond Hall. Stow Lake, for example, has become one of the park's most beautiful features. Yet in safeguarding for the future the incomparable natural resources of Golden Gate Park, San Franciscans might do well to consider Hall's philosophy: "The value of a park consists of its being a park . . ." not a civic center or an amusement zone but a place of access to nature, a refuge from the pressures of city life. There can be little doubt what Hall's reaction would be to recurring proposals for freeways through the park. It is not hard to imagine the park's wrathful founder on some Elysian cloud, preparing to hurl his jovian thunderbolts at the latest invaders of his green sanctuary.

The McLaren Legend

John McLaren's first major job when he began work at the park in 1887 under Hall was to carry out Hall's plan for a large children's playground near the southeast corner of the park. Hall's idea for the "Children's Quarter," as he called it (now often mislabeled "Childrens Quarters," as if it were a barracks), was a pioneering project; even Olmsted had not thought of it. Millionaire William Sharon, Ralston's partner, put up most of the money, including funds for "Sharon Cottage," a brownstone recreation building which appears much the same as the day it was finished, as does most of the playground itself.

When McLaren took over as Superintendent in 1889 after Hall's second resignation, he had the benefit of Commissioner Stow's long experience as the most powerful man in Sacramento. Even Hall admitted, despite his distaste for Stow, that the former railroad attorney was able to raise the park's income to the point where McLaren could repair the damage that had been done during the Dark Decade of neglect. McLaren's own taste in parks was similar to Hall's; he preferred trees to tennis courts and meadows to museums. But he was more flexible than Hall and felt obliged to accept sport facilities, statues, buildings, and other "improvements" as the price of getting the budget he wanted for his beloved trees. When influential park commissioners wanted to put a mile-long "speedway" in the park to accommodate their friends in the horsy set, McLaren grudgingly went along, and was bitterly criticized by Hall, in private, for doing so. Later, when a regular three-quarter-mile oval horse track, polo field, and stadium were built (Adolph Spreckels was the chief benefactor), the speedway was converted into Speedway Meadow and West Speedway Meadow, interrupted midway by the new track. But even the new polo-field complex did not satisfy the sporting crowd; it was in a windy location and too far from the streetcar lines. So McLaren had to stomach another "compromise"— Kezar Stadium, which took over the location not only of the park nursery but a rhododendron dell he had carefully landscaped and nurtured over the decades until it was the nation's finest display of the colorful plants.

"Uncle John" salvaged two minor triumphs from the defeat, however. He convinced the city to buy some adjacent property as part of the stadium site in order to diminish the effect on the park. And he had something to say about the layout of the stadium. The promoters intended to build the field running north and south, as most stadiums are laid out, in order that the spectators on one side would not be facing the sun all day. But to do so in this case would nearly have bisected the park. Kezar was built in 1924, runs east and west, and sunburnt spectators can thank McLaren.

Innumerable tales have been told about McLaren's practice of planting vegetation around the park's statues to hide them, his mobilization of his gardeners to defend the park from would-be developers, his aversion to "Keep Off the Grass" signs, his feuds with politicians and promoters. Many of the stories have doubtless been embellished in several generations of retelling. But he was the type of man around whom a body of legend inevitably grows up, and to admit that he was not always successful in repelling invasions of the park is not to disparage his place in San Francisco's history as one of the city's undisputed heroes, one of the last in the line of giants who left an indelible mark on this city from Brannan to Ralston to Hall to Rolph to Giannini.

Uncle John's Rocks

McLaren's preference for the works of nature over the structures of man was qualified by one glaring idiosynacrasy. He had a low opinion of nature's rocks, felt that they were not adequate to his landscaping purposes, and was fond of improving on them by providing rocks of his own. As a result, throughout the park the visitor with a sharp eye often does a double take. What appear to be natural boulders may be artfully devised concrete imitations, sometimes joining smaller natural rocks, sometimes as completely fabricated as the outdoor scenery on the back lot at M-G-M. This procedure was a virtual necessity in such locations as the cliff below Sutro Heights opposite the Cliff House, where the crumbly rock is held in place by a concrete escarpment natural enough to deceive all but the most discerning.

Park employees who worked for McLaren remember him as a kindly tyrant who on the surface was sometimes more tyrannical than kindly. His standards were exacting; on more than one occasion when he found that a tree had not been planted on precisely the right spot, he required the gardeners to dig it up and replant it, sometimes a few inches away. One such tree was an Atlas cedar that still stands inside the park's Nineteenth Avenue gate.

Assistant Superintendent Roy Hudson described a similar incident that occurred to him at another location. "I knew that tree was centered in exactly the right spot," he says. "I had measured it out to the inch, but Mr. McLaren ordered me to replant it anyhow." Hudson noticed that the tree was a little bushier on one side than on the other, which might have given it the appearance of being off center. So instead of replanting it he trimmed it carefully to make it more symmetrical and scuffed up the ground roundabout to make the surface appear as if it had been dug up.

"The next day when Uncle John came around he looked over the tree and told me I had done a good job," says Hudson. "He didn't say another word. But I didn't fool him for a minute. He knew exactly what I had done and went along with me on it."

McLaren demanded obedience, but he respected people who did not kowtow to him. On one occasion he took Hudson to task for some minor matter, and Hudson, who was convinced that the boss was wrong, told him so in emphatic terms. McLaren's chauffeur warned him to go easy on the old man, who at that point was nearing ninety. Hudson stalked off, wondering whether he had lost his job. The next day the chauffeur told him that McLaren's car had a flat tire and asked Hudson to drive the boss in his own car on a trip to one of the outlying parks.

"I was suspicious," Hudson recalls. "I looked at that car, and there was no flat tire. So I drove McLaren down there, half expecting to be fired on the way. He didn't mention the argument at all. We had a long talk. Or rather he talked and I listened. He told me about his plans and ideas. It was one of the few times he ever really opened up to me. Then as we approached the end of the tour he reached over and put his hand on my knee: 'My boy,' he said, 'when you're right don't let anyone talk you out of it. But be sure you're right!' "

Uncle John was on the job until the last months of his life. After he died in 1943 at the age of ninety-six, Hudson and the park staff developed John McLaren Memorial Rhododendron Dell—four acres of McLaren's favorite plants in a landscaped area so natural and tranquil that even William Hammond Hall would have approved of it.

Mike de Young's Gamble

M. H. de Young, founder of the *Chronicle*, returned home from the Chicago Columbian Exposition of 1893 with a wild idea that appealed to the reckless instincts of a generation not far removed from the halcyon days of the Mother Lode and the Comstock. At the bottom of a depression that had closed banks by the dozen, de Young proposed that San Francisco take the offensive and stimulate business by putting on an exposition of its own, borrowing exhibits from the closed-down Chicago fair and calling attention to this city's salubrious climate by holding the outdoor show in the middle of the winter.

The Midwinter Fair was staged in Golden Gate Park and opened its gates in January 1894, featuring, among other attractions from Chicago, the blaring band of John Philip Sousa and a landscaped "Japanese Village," representing the exotic new country that had recently been "opened" to the West. The garden was designed by George Turner Marsh, owner of America's first oriental art goods store, then located in the original Palace Hotel, now on Sutter Street.

De Young's gamble paid off. The fair was successful; the Japanese Village turned out to be a genuine attraction and so delighted San Franciscans that they decided to make it a permanent feature of the park. On McLaren's recommendation the management was taken over by Makoto Hagiwara, scion of a prominent family in Japan. Hagiwara had come to California in 1870, had gone to work as a cook and dishwasher, and in the following quarter century had become a successful San Francisco restaurateur.

In the Japanese Village, which he converted into a tea garden, he found an ideal outlet for his artistic energies and his love of natural greenery. He was happy as long as he could operate the garden in his own way, but in 1900, when Golden Gate Park was transferred from state to the city, Hagiwara feuded with city officials, moved out, and set up his own Japanese Village across from the park. The park's tea garden deteriorated until in 1910 the city relented and asked Hagiwara to come back, turning the garden over to him completely as a concession. He build a Japanese-style house there for living quarters and put his whole family to work.

The arrangement was hardly a money-making operation; out of the revenue from selling tea and rice cakes, Hagiwara had to pay the city fifty dollars a month for the concession, support his family, and maintain the garden. Doubtless he dipped into his own pocket frequently to finance the garden, and his rewards had to come in the acclaim of visitors from around the world. The garden was expanded and ponds were developed. A high-arching "Moon Bridge" was built—designed, among other reasons, to slow visitors down. Hagiwara wanted to make it difficult for people to rush through his garden. Another feature was designed for a similar purpose—a steep stairway leading up to a multiroofed pagoda, which the garden had acquired from the Panama-Pacific Exposition of 1915. Traditionally the "penance" stairs are so designed to cause anyone approaching a temple to pause at each step to catch his breath and utter a prayer before proceeding. In the Japanese view, it is impossible to enjoy nature or be properly reverent in a hurry.

The Return of the Tea Garden

Over the years Makoto Hagiwara made several trips to his native land, each time bringing back special plants, trees and art objects for the garden, stone lanterns, statuary, rocks, and the greatest prizes of all—bonsai trees, which

131

were dwarfed, carefully trimmed, deliberately kept small to fit the Japanese concept of planned landscapes as symbolic miniatures of natural wilderness. When Makoto Hagiwara died in 1925, his son Goro took over and carried on the garden until his own death twelve years later. Goro Hagiwara's wife then assumed management, aided by her daughter Sumi and her son George, who in 1935 had rebuilt the original teahouse in permanent form.

After Pearl Harbor the Hagiwaras—and the garden—were hit by a shattering blow. Pacific coast residents who had the misfortune to have Japanese ancestry were ordered to leave the coast. The Hagiwara widow and her children, all of them native American citizens, were stunned by the evacuation order. Most of their personal property was in the garden—the investment of three generations. Bewildered by the turn of events, they began to pack up their hundreds of potted plants and art objects, wondering what could be done with them. Under Army orders, the evacuees had five months to settle their business and get out, but city officials, irate at the Hagiwaras for claiming their property, ordered the family to leave the park even earlier. John McLaren, who had stood by the Hagiwaras, was out of the picture by this time.

An acquaintance of the Hagiwaras came to the rescue. Samuel Newsom, who had lived for several years in Japan studying Japanese gardens, offered to hold the Hagiwara collection for safekeeping at his nursery in Mill Valley. So the family sadly packed up the stone lanterns, potted plants, and shallow-rooted shrubs, the dwarf Japanese maples and the ancient bonsai trees that the elder Hagiwaras had brought from Japan over the years, and loaded them onto trucks for Mill Valley. At the urging of park officials they left behind some fifty potted plants in order to avoid stripping the garden bare, although the city never saw fit to pay for the property. And the Japanese Tea Garden became the Oriental Tea Garden for the duration of the war.

After the war, members of the Hagiwara family again applied for the concession, but the city's terms were too tough. Reluctantly, they sold their collection, and most of it was ultimately acquired by Dr. Hugh Fraser of Oakland. With the Hagiwara collection as a nucleus, Fraser and his wife developed one of the outstanding Japanese gardens in the United States. The couple decided that the Hagiwara property should eventually be returned to Golden Gate Park, along with their own extensive collection. After

Mrs. Fraser died, her husband, carrying out the terms of his wife's will, presented the combined collections to the city as a memorial to his wife and appropriately hired as designer the Hagiwara's old benefactor, Sam Newsom, now owner of the Greenwood Tree, an oriental goods store in Mill Valley; author of several books on Japanese gardens; and one of the nation's ranking authorities on the subject.

George Hagiwara, who was raised in the tea garden, again lives in San Francisco but seldom visits the garden; he finds the memories too painful. But he expressed his appreciation to Dr. Fraser and went to the park to watch Newsom landscape the area, happy to see the return of some of the old familiar bonsai trees, plants and art objects brought here by his father and grandfather. The newly designed area was dedicated at cherry blossom time in April 1966. Although observers at the dedication saw several plaques and memorials in the garden, nowhere was there any mention of the Hagiwara family. It would seem that, after a quarter century, San Francisco is long overdue in making amends for its shabby treatment of the family that for three generations dedicated its unflagging energies to the development of this renowned gem of landscape art.

High Wilderness

At the opposite end of nature's spectrum from the meticulously planned, immaculately manicured Tea Garden is a well-nigh impenetrable wilderness, a forest in the middle of the city. If you live near the geographic center of San Francisco, you can hear its sound on windy nights like the roar of the surf in a winter storm. The noise comes from above, booming down out of the sky, and one half expects to see the Wagnerian Valkyries galloping across the heavens. It is high on Mount Sutro and, primeval though the forest appears today, is as man-made as the Tea Garden. It was planted by Adolph Sutro, a man who himself thundered across the stage of nineteenth-century San Francisco like a giant wind.

Sutro's trees, untended for more than half a century, have reverted to a jungle inhabited principally by raccoons, skunks, and domestic cats turned wild. Actually he intended this and his other tree plantations to be landscaped pleasure grounds for San Franciscans, arboreal oases on this almost treeless, windswept peninsula.

133

It seems oddly symbolic that his gardens have turned to jungle, for beneath Sutro's cultivated urbanity, his love of learning and the arts, he possessed—or was possessed by—a compulsive drive consisting of raw, primitive energy and an almost demonic passion for power. In this respect he was typical of nineteenth-century San Francisco itself—a combination of lusty frontier vitality and cosmopolitan sophistication. Sutro's historic achievement (long before he planted the forest) was one of the engineering wonders of the nineteenth century—a four-mile tunnel through a mountain to drain and provide better access to the fabulous silver mines of the Comstock Lode in Nevada. After innumerable setbacks, extending construction over a decade, he finished the job in 1879, then returned to San Francisco to look for new outlets for his energies.

Everything he tackled he did with might, main strength, and runaway power. He went into real estate and bought up one twelfth of the area of San Francisco. He collected books and accumulated the biggest and most valuable library of rare volumes in the West. He conceived the idea of planting trees on San Francisco's barren hills, and before he was through he had set out more than a million saplings, foresting acre after acre with the botanical fervor of a dozen Johnny Appleseeds.

Hoping to instill an equivalent zeal for forestation in the younger generation, he initiated the city's first Arbor Day, characteristically not with a simple tree-planting ceremony but with an extravaganza and a cast of thousands. On a November morning in 1886 several thousand schoolchildren and their parents took ferries to Yerba Buena Island and marched up the hill in a long procession led by a brass band. Dignitaries, including old General Vallejo, delivered orations; poet Joaquin Miller recited some verses composed for the occasion ("Against our goldened orient lawns/We lift a living light today . . ."); and Sutro himself set out the first sapling, with a sonorous oration prophesying that under these trees on the anniversary of this Arbor Day a century hence homage would be paid to the planters.

Then the children went to work and set out thousands of trees on a plot the shape of a cross and twice the length of a football field. The youngsters were also given saplings to take home, and doubtless many a big Monterey pine and eucalyptus still standing in San Francisco backyards today stems from Sutro's expansive vision of residential districts wooded like the Forest of Arden. Similar plantings inspired by Sutro took place in the Presidio, where the groves still stand in regimental rows as they were conscientiously set out by the schoolchildren.

The biggest forest of all was on Sutro's own property on the old Rancho San Miguel, including Mount Parnassus, later known as Mount Sutro. From Sutro's nursery near Laguna Honda, his battalions of workmen planted blue-gum eucalyptus, pines, cypresses, acacias, ashes, beeches, and maples by the tens of thousands. From the foot of the hill near the present site of the University of California Medical Center, Sutro's woods swept up and over both of the peak's summits, down to the lake at Laguna Honda, and up toward another massive stand on the city's highest point at Mount Davidson —all part of the Rancho. Some of his plantings remain in the Forest Hill district, the city's only wooded neighborhood.

Within the past decade Sutro Forest has been diminished to a fraction of its original size, retreating on the south and west before subdivisions and on the north before the advance of the University of California Medical Center, which owns most of the remaining woods except for a city-owned strip on the east. The University has made imaginative use of portions of the forest, however, particularly in Aldea San Miguel, the student housing area off Clarendon, and there are plans for further landscaping of the upper slopes, now largely impenetrable.

Long gone are the paths, lookout points, and rustic bridges Sutro built for the recreation and inspiration of the masses. Gone, too, are most of the varieties of trees he planted, driven out, in the absence of care, by the aggressive blue gums, except where an occasional Monterey pine or cypress has managed to survive. The ground is covered with dense thickets of thorny blackberry and poison oak. But walk on Mount Sutro when the wind is roaring through the forest; a hundred thousand eucalyptus are bending before the blast, their trunks and limbs vibrating like an aeolian harp; and you can feel in your innards the driving fury of the giant who pierced a mountain with the world's greatest tunnel. At such times, the King of the Comstock still stalks these heights.

Birthplace of the City

The last of the visible sand dunes on which most of San Francisco was built can still be seen at Fort Funston State Park in the southwestern corner

135

of the city, where you will have a hard time finding the fortifications, now mercifully disguised by nature. The "ice plant" covering these dunes is so thick in places that you can't avoid treading on it, and it feels springy and spongy underfoot. In other areas the sand is bare, and your feet slide as you walk down the dunes or, as you climb, slip backward a few inches with each step.

Immediately to the west, beyond the cliffs that drop off to the beach, the sunlight wells up from the ocean. Long green swells appear a quarter mile offshore, grow in height until they are top-heavy and curl over into white foam with a resounding boom. It was waves like these, rolling from distant storms in the long millenniums before the coming of man, that carved these cliffs and shaped the site on which the city stands. You can hear their roar among the dunes and smell their salt fragrance on the breeze, mixed with the aroma of the sage.

Small yellow and white and red butterflies flutter among the dune grasses in the autumn sunshine. Big white gulls and graceful terns soar above the cliffs where they can catch the updrafts off the ocean. The low mesembry-anthemum, rolling over the dunes, forms a ground cover of many colors, from greens in the small valleys and swales to reds and oranges in the drier zones on top of the dunes. As you glimpse one sand ridge against the sun it appears to be ablaze with the brilliant red of these plants, spreading along the crest of the dune like a running ground fire. There are other colors in the dunes—the pale green leaves of the lupine bushes that in spring will flower into yellow, the scarlet of Indian paintbrush, the gold of poppies, the lavender of sea asters and small sand verbenas.

In the smooth sand where the dunes are bare you can see the curving patterns of ripples spread by the wind and the fine tracings of tracks left by the dunes' inhabitants—lizards, rabbits, ground squirrels. In sheltered vales are low cypresses, weathered and gnarled like those on the coast near Carmel. Hidden among the dunes like ancient ruins are the remains of concrete blockhouses and gun emplacements, left over from the time when this area was fortified. Named for General Frederick Funston, Army commander at the Presidio during the disaster of 1906, the fort functioned as part of the now-obsolete coastal defenses. From the dune tops you can see the long strand of Ocean Beach stretching five miles north to the Cliff House, the rolling slopes of the Sunset and Richmond districts rising to

Twin Peaks and Mount Davidson, the nearby shores and blue waters of Lake Merced.

Closer by are the geologic clues to what happened here in past ages. The oldest rock visible here is the stratified Merced formation, named for the lake, where it was discovered. You can see it in dark-colored veins running through the sandy cliffs and in outcrops along the beach below. These strata, deposited on top of the older Franciscan formation, consist mostly of clay, shale, sandstone, pebbles, and shells laid down on the bottom of an ancient sea that covered this area possibly two million years ago. But part of the topmost layer (the latest to be deposited) consists of the kind of stone and sand laid down by fresh-water streams or brackish marshes.

Thus it is clear that this area was under the ocean at the beginning of the Merced formation and later received stream deposits—evidence that the land was rising out of the sea and that these peninsular hills were taking shape. At some later point in geologic time there was a buckling of the earth's crust, causing the Merced strata to be tilted sharply downward toward the present site of Lake Merced to the northeast, a tilt readily visible in the exposed outcrops along the beach. The lake did not yet exist, but the tilt prepared the way for it, and later erosion created a valley there.

During the big thaw at the end of the last Ice Age, beginning some fifteen thousand years ago, the ocean flooded into the mouth of the Merced Valley, creating an inlet or small bay—a "drowned valley" in the geologist's language. It was this same rise in sea level that caused the ocean to flood through the Golden Gate and invade the much larger valley of the Sacramento River, creating San Francisco Bay.

The ocean, raised to new heights, battered the edge of the land, gouging away quantities of soil, sand, and rocks, creating the cliffs that stretch south from this point. The soil, sand, and rocks ripped away from the cliffs were ground into fine particles by the power of the waves and carried in the direction of the prevailing longshore current—to the north. As the sand-laden current moved across the mouth of the flooded Merced Valley, it deposited part of its load as a sand bar, which in time extended entirely across the entrance to the inlet, damming it off from the ocean. Streams flowing into the drowned valley eventually replaced the salt water with fresh, creating today's Lake Merced.

The waves and currents, continuing to deposit the sand along the shore to the north, created over the millenniums the long strand of Ocean Beach. Here, where the breakers boom and the shorebirds ride the wind currents, you can still see the elements of the geologic process that gave birth to the contours of the land on which the city stands—the cliffs, the beach, the built-over dunes rising to the central hills.

Rim of the Continent

Doubtless there are few cities where it is possible to take an eight-mile walk in a straight line uninterrupted by streets, structures, or traffic, along a natural avenue where the works of man, if visible at all, can be seen only in the remote distance, and the overwhelming presence is that of nature itself. There is no finer walking anywhere than at low tide along Ocean Beach, longest and narrowest of the city's parks, where you can examine the flotsam of the sea, watch the waves, trace the markings of the water on the sand, or simply think private thoughts against a backdrop of elemental forces.

The city's ocean border is about five miles long, but the beach continues for another three miles south of the city line. Perhaps the most impressive way to approach it is through Golden Gate Park, where it seems always a surprise to walk along a path over thickly wooded hillocks and suddenly confront the ocean. One day in December I emerged from the woods, crossed the road, and found that a minus tide had left the beach particularly broad and flat. Flocks of gulls stood on sand bars one hundred yards out, mirrored upside down on the glistening surface. The conditions of sand and tide seemed ideal to explore the rocks at the foot of the Cliff House, so I walked north along the flat, springy beach, observing the herringbone swash marks on the sand and the remains of sand dollars cast up by the recent storm.

I remembered that some years ago at another time when the tide was extraordinarily low and the height of the sand was exactly right, I had come upon some normally inaccessible caverns extending back into the rock beneath the Cliff House. Exploring now the foot of the cliff and keeping a wary eye out for recurrent high waves, I discovered again the entrance to one of the caves, well hidden back among the recesses of the wall. Probing cautiously inside, I found that the narrow portal opened up into a large

138

chamber with a high-vaulted ceiling. The far walls were invisible in the darkness. The grotto resounded like a colossal conch shell echoing the roar of the waves outside.

As my eyes grew accustomed to the gloom, I found I was standing on the edge of a quiet pool. I tossed a few handfuls of sand into the dark but could not determine the location of the far shore. Curiously, at that moment, my mind went back through the decades to a long-forgotten episode from the Oz books I had read as a youngster. *The Scarecrow of Oz* opened, I recalled, near the Cliff House, where L. Frank Baum's characters, an old salt called Cap'n Bill and a young girl named Trot, somehow became trapped in such a grotto as this, went through a pool, followed a tunnel and found their way, ultimately, after innumerable adventures, to the Land of Oz.

Unwilling to venture into the mysterious pool, I may have passed up a splendid opportunity. I remembered, however, that on my last trip here I had found another cavern, which as I recalled had branched off to the left of this one. It was a narrow tunnel, and I had followed it back into the rock, groping in the blackness around some turns until I feared getting lost in these lightless catacombs—like Tom Sawyer in his cave—and had retreated to daylight. Now I looked around again for the tunnel, exploring all the crevices from which it might have opened up, but it was nowhere to be found. Evidently it had been sealed off by deposits of sand and was open only on rare occasions when the sand was shifted by the waves. Conceivably I had seen the entrance the only time it had been open since Cap'n Bill and Trot made their trip to Oz.

I continued to skirt the cliff, peering back into the recesses, finding smaller caves, including one which opened up to the sky straight above as if it were the bottom of a well. I was expecting my journey to be ended at points where previously I had always encountered deep water at the foot of the cliff, but as I raced a wave around one point I found to my surprise that I was in the cove beyond the Cliff House. It was the first time in my experience that the beach route had been traversable the entire distance. I walked past the giant decaying hulk of Sutro Baths and investigated an acre-sized rock to the left, where the waves reverberated in watery passages visible only at this extreme low tide. Flickering lights, refracted through submarine windows, cast a green glow in dim tunnels, and big crabs scuttled among the crevices.

Finally reaching a place where the waves prevented further beach-level walking, I climbed up a rocky point, passing a man-made pool designed by Adolph Sutro in the 1890s to catch the wave spray and reveal the wonders of tide-pool life. From a point above the pool I could look down into Needle Cove, where the low water revealed some oddly shaped, half-submerged forms. They were covered with algae and barnacles, and at first glance appeared to be offshore rocks, but their contours were too regular, too smoothly curving, to be completely natural. Then I noticed what appeared to be the mast or stem of a ship protruding from the water nearby, and I realized that I was looking at the remains of the freighter *Ohioan* that went aground here nearly thirty years ago and was soon pounded to pieces by the waves.

Here, on the westernmost point of mainland San Francisco, was impressive evidence of the power of the ocean—in the sunken freighter; in the battered outposts of Seal Rocks and other sea stacks that had once been part of this coast but were cut off by millennial wave assault; in the sea-designed architecture of these sandstone cliffs, changing form and retreating sporadically before the attacks of the Pacific. The waves were doing their work as I watched, pounding like battering rams at the rock wall, eroding it away grain by grain in the perennial contest between the ocean and the land.

Leaning back against the cliff, I could almost feel the mass of the continent behind me and sense the upheavals of the earth that had raised this rock from the sea bottom, the onslaught of the ocean that was wearing it away into the sea bottom once more, the titanic geologic forces that would presumably, after uncounted eons, thrust it again to the surface. And, where in these dizzying cycles of time, I wondered, was the place for this city at the continent's edge—and the race of beings who built it? Doubtless long after the volatile homo sapiens had disappeared, the more durable species—the barnacles and the crabs and the mussels—would still cling to the rocks where the land and the sea come together.

A particularly big wave exploded on the rock base below and sent a shower of spray over me. I quickly scrambled down and headed back the way I had come before the rising tide could again seal off the route at the foot of the cliffs.

Monterey cypresses dominate Speedway Meadow in Golden Gate Park. This was one end of an old horse-racing track a straight mile long. The far end of the track is now West Speedway Meadow, out of sight just beyond the Polo Field, which is visible in the distance.

Some of the city's waterways have historic importance. The Chain of Lakes, ABOVE, is where park founder William Hammond Hall discovered the plant that he subsequently sowed to hold the sand, enabling him eventually to plant the eucalyptus and pine woodland that has replaced the dunes. Mountain Lake, BELOW, was the first campsite of the Anza expedition that founded San Francisco in 1776, and Father Font noted in his diary that at that time there was not a tree in sight.

The spring pictured here is in the Presidio and was known to the Spaniards as El Polin. The Indians believed that its waters were miraculous, and the Spaniards carried on the tradition. Maidens who drank from the spring in the full of the moon, it was believed, were assured of many children and eternal bliss, although it is difficult to understand how they could have both.

The visitors to Golden Gate Park who see only the portion of the landscape alongside the roads miss at least half of the park's attractions. Exploration by foot reveals the hidden beauty of quiet vales and dells inaccessible by any other means. One such place is De Laveaga Dell, where in the autumn the yellow leaves of the big elms fall among the rhododendrons and ferns and float on the surface of the still waters.

Another is Quarry Lake, where the dark red chert beds that underlie the sand are revealed in an old quarry escarpment, gnarled roots of Monterey pines twist eloquently over the strata, and giant tree ferns from an early era of evolution give the vale an antediluvian atmosphere. You almost expect to see a pterodactyl swoop through the ancient trees to the lake. To students of paleontology and plant evolution the Quarry Lake area so resembles an early period of earth history that they call it Tertiary Valley.

This might be a scene from the redwood country of northern California, but it is a grove of Strybing Arboretum in Golden Gate Park, planted in 1889 by John McLaren and maintained in indigenous fashion by P. H. "Jock" Brydon, the arboretum's present director and spiritual descendant of McLaren. Beneath the big trees are plants native to the redwood region, including chain fern (*Wood-wardia*) and the cloverlike redwood sorrel.

The Japanese Tea Garden is the most popular natural feature of Golden Gate Park, particularly in March and April when the pink and white cherry blossoms fill the garden with the essence of spring. Adults as well as children love to scramble up and down the steep Moon Bridge and watch their reflections in the water.

146

Nowhere is spring more exhilarating than among the rhododendrons of Golden Gate Park. You will miss John McLaren Memorial Rhododendron Dell if you don't get out of the car and stroll down the winding paths through the four acres of plants eight and ten feet high with masses of blossoms the size of a man's head. There are pinks and whites and lavenders that will remind you of girls in summer dresses. And beware of the reds! Some of them make an assault on the optic nerve that might have a traumatic effect.

The big showy flowers are natives of the Himalayan foothills but seem very much at home here. McLaren Dell, really several dells and hillocks, has been laid out with such ingenuity and imagination that the whole design—like the best art of any kind—seems natural and not contrived. The flowers grow rhythmically through dale and swale beneath Monterey pines and cypresses and eucalyptuses. There are other flowers too, low-growing azaleas in warm yellows and oranges like a creeping flame, cyclamens like fires of red and purple, luminous masses of forget-me-nots that shine like sunlight on blue water.

The impresario of this floral extravaganza is Assistant Superintendent Roy Hudson, who developed the dell in the 1940s, after the death of "Uncle John," as a memorial to his chief.

The principal "shrub" in Golden Gate Park is really a tree—the *Leptospermum,* the Australian "tea tree." Captain Cook's men discovered that its leaves had a fine flavor when used to brew the English national beverage. Like the live oak, the tea tree grows more horizontally than vertically and sometimes leans so far that it rests on the ground. The fine flowing textures of its bark accentuate the intricate contortions of the trunk. John McLaren planted these trees in the dunes by the thousands, along with beach grass, lupine, and *Acacia longifolia,* to help hold the drifting sand.

For many years this hill at the north end of Golden Gate Heights was an enclave of nature in a crowded neighborhood. It had been formed in past ages by sand drifting up from the ocean around outcrops of dark red chert, which were still visible. Long ago someone had planted eucalyptus, Monterey pines, and cypresses, and there were sloping acres of sand and soil covered by grasses and chaparral, bright in season with sweet alyssum, yellow lupine, goldenrod, Indian paintbrush, California poppies, and a dozen other varieties of wildflowers.

This green oasis attracted wildlife in abundance, including a dozen species of birds— quail, red-shafted flickers, white-crowned sparrows, various woodpeckers. Doves and a pair of red-tailed hawks nested in these trees.

Then in the spring of 1966, when these pictures were taken, the men with the bulldozers arrived and began to topple the trees and rip up the hill. The land had become too valuable to lie "idle" any longer. No one was able to envision this invaluable area as a nature preserve, where adults as well as schoolchildren could study the lessons of nature and enjoy the matchless panoramas. A large part of the hill was graded down and sold off to fatten the pocketbooks of developers, all in the name of progress.

Part Four

THE WILDLIFE

The Nocturnalists

The census takers probably overlook at least as many San Franciscans as they count. It is a good bet that the human residents of this crowded city are outnumbered by the wild animals. In fact, there are probably more species of wildlife in the city now than were here before the coming of the white man. Some, it is true, have disappeared: the fearsome grizzly that was more numerous on the peninsula south of San Francisco than anywhere else in the state; the friendly, intelligent sea otters that thronged these waters by the hundreds of thousands and were killed off by the most ferocious predator of all—man (they have made a comeback in the Monterey area and there are occasional unverified reports of otter off Land's End); the deer and elk that were chased with little success over the hills by the soldiers of Portolá and Anza and departed for the wilder areas of the peninsula when the city became too crowded. But the Americans came to these dunes, planted their trees and created habitats that were not here before, attracting such new residents as robins and juncos, who would never be caught dead on a sand dune but who love to roost in the Monterey pines and cypresses; and raccoons, who also are not fond of dunes and came up the peninsula to live in the thick woods of Sutro Forest, Golden Gate Park, and the Presidio. Such species as eastern gray squirrels and possums came from other parts of the country; they probably escaped or were released from captivity.

The mammals are seldom visible in the daytime. Most of them prefer to hunt at night, but you can see ample evidence of their nocturnal activities any morning in such areas as Golden Gate Park. The raccoons, possums, and weasels dig up the lawns, searching for burrowing mice and other rodents, and are particularly the despair of golf-course keepers. Even more of a problem than gophers are the moles, who not only dig holes and leave mounds of piled earth over the entrance (molehills which appear mountainous to a gardener) but also plow up the surface with long shallow tunnels as they hunt for worms and insects. The mole is about the size of a gopher, and like his arrogant-looking, buck-toothed counterpart, appears to be something dreamed up in the imagination of a comic-strip artist. His eyes and ears are normally covered by fur, which lies in either direction, so that he can scoot either backward or forward in his tight tunnels. From the fur protrudes a long burrowing snout. Two big front feet, facing sideward, plow the earth like a swimmer doing the breaststroke—and at about the same speed.

Doubtless the most glamorous of the city's mammals, though far from the most numerous, are the native gray foxes. One den of foxes has sometimes been spotted in an area adjacent to the most populous part of Golden Gate Park; one colony in the Presidio sometimes explores a nearby residential district; and there have at times been several dens of them around the cliffs and chaparral-covered slopes of Land's End. They help keep down the rodent and rabbit population, but unlike the digging mammals are harmless to the landscape and vegetation. The grays are the only tree-climbing foxes and may hop into the branches of a live oak to escape dogs or just to have a look around.

The rabbits most likely to be seen in brushy areas of the city, from McLaren Park to Land's End, are, appropriately enough, brush rabbits, closely related to the familiar cottontail. Occasionally a leggy jack rabbit (which is not really a rabbit but a hare) can be seen galloping along a road or parkway. No coyotes have been spotted within the city limits for many years, and no wildcats, although Golden Gate Park has a population of domestic cats who have heard the call of the wild and make a comfortable living off the park's rodent and bird population.

There is a full-time "hunter" on the park staff, whose job is to reduce the populations of rodents and digging mammals. Larger mammals, such as raccoons, he traps and delivers to the SPCA, although he carries a shotgun and is permitted to blast away at the coots or mudhens, whose assiduous digging for worms can completely destroy a lawn.

Some years ago a young boy walking home from school daily along the Lyon Street steps next to the Presidio made friends with a small mammal by giving it left-overs from his lunch. Ultimately he used the same lure to entice the animal home, thinking it might make a good pet. His parents took one look and demurred; the pet was a shiny, black-and-white *Mephitis mephitis*, more commonly known as a striped skunk. These engaging animals are fairly common throughout the city, probably more so than the smaller spotted skunk. The former has a single white stripe running from head to tail for a total length of two feet or more. He gives fair warning before he strikes, raising his tail and drumming on the ground with his front feet, curving with head and tail pointed toward his enemy. Then he fires his aromatic charge of oil from beneath his tail and can aim with accuracy up to ten or twelve feet—or even twenty feet with a good tail wind. He only has five or six shots available for one firing but they are usually more than enough.

The western spotted skunk is less than half the size of his striped cousin but his chief weapon is equally potent. He has several white stripes running both vertically and horizontally, often broken into spots, and an odd habit of doing a graceful handstand, sometimes just for pleasure, sometimes for a better aim when he is about to fire. The spotted skunk is more jovial than his bigger relative, and when deodorized makes a pet as playful as a kitten. In Golden Gate Park skunks favor the Japanese Tea Garden, where after hours they can gather a succulent meal of cookie crumbs left by teahouse patrons. Traps set beneath the teahouse have bagged as many as thirteen at once.

The Passing of the "Seals"

Although the city's skunks, foxes, weasels, possums, and raccoons have adapted well to the coming of man—and some may even have increased their numbers—the same, unfortunately, cannot be said for the most famed

152

of San Francisco's mammals, the "seals" of Seal Rocks, which are not seals at all but sea lions. The seals, which prefer isolated sandy beaches, disappeared from the shores of the city (although they are still occasionally seen in the water) when the beaches ceased to be isolated. Sea lions, however, are fond of making their homes on offshore rocks and islands, and they traditionally congregated by the hundreds on the big rocks off the Cliff House. They once used the rocks for breeding purposes, but have not done so since the rookeries there were raided by commercial hunters beginning in 1860. For the breeding season in spring they migrate fifty miles south to Año Nuevo Island or seaward twenty-five miles to the Farallones. A mighty uproar takes place at the rookery when the big bulls battle for their harems, rounding up ten or fifteen cows apiece.

Customarily they returned to Seal Rocks in late summer or early fall, but in recent years the population there has steadily diminished, and visitors continually raise the query: "Where are the sea lions?" The answer is that they have probably gone to Año Nuevo or Point Reyes or the Farallones to get away from it all—from the fishing boats that hover off the rocks in increasing numbers, from the nuisance of low-flying helicopters, and from the surfers who frequent the area just inshore and sometimes paddle on their boards out to the rocks to explore. Nowadays Seal Rocks are no longer a home for the animals but merely a stop-off point where a few—possibly a dozen at a time or occasionally several dozen—will haul ashore for a time before swimming on.

The species that once inhabited these rocks in great numbers was the Steller sea lion, named for biologist Georg Steller. This is a beefy animal weighing up to a ton and emitting a roar as impressive as that of the land lion. The fearsome sound arising from Seal Rocks provided early-day navigators with a natural fog horn, officially recommended by the Coast Guard. In recent years the Steller sea lions have been seen on the rocks in the company of their smaller cousins, the California sea lions, whose normal habitat is farther south. The latter are about one third the size of the Stellers, are darker brown in color, and bark rather than roar. One theory for their appearance here and elsewhere on the central California coast is that the species shifted its range northward when its Baja California habitat became the hunting grounds of a dog-food manufacturer.

Probably no wild mammal makes himself at home in the city with the ease and savoir faire of the raccoon. He makes forays from all the natural areas, Golden Gate Park, the Presidio, and particularly Sutro Forest, into the surrounding neighborhoods, and residents hearing the familiar midnight rattle of garbage lids can expect to find raccoon tracks the next morning. Consistent with his reputation for washing all his food thoroughly, he is usually neat about his business, seldom overturns the can and scatters the garbage, and sometimes even carefully replaces the lid. He may make himself at home not only in the city but in your house as well. Residents around Sutro Forest sometimes find the big, hollow-eyed mammal, weighing in at thirty pounds or more, staring in the window or rapping at the door, demanding a handout, or even walking through an open door to help himself to the larder. He will steer clear of dogs if possible, but often outwits the canines if an encounter cannot be avoided. Raccoons have been known to lead a pursuing dog into the water, climb on its head and drown it.

Raccoons have commonly been found as far from natural areas as Russian Hill, and they regularly raided fishponds of residents there until the old reservoir at the top of Hyde Street was covered over a few years ago and the water-loving animals moved elsewhere. Actually a body of water is not essential to the raccoon, and although he often does prefer to wash his food in a pond if possible, sometimes he will "wash" it in mud or sand. Biologists believe that he is less interested in cleanliness than he might seem; his long dextrous fingers are sensitive and he simply enjoys feeling his meal as well as smelling and tasting it.

Theme and Variations

For most San Franciscans the principal contact with wildlife comes via the ear. Most mammals roam only when the human population is normally asleep; birds are often well hidden in the vegetation; but wherever there are trees or shrubs the sounds of wildness issue forth for all to hear, in songs or calls, in pipings and chatterings and trumpetings, particularly in the spring but to some degree at any time of the year. The perceptive ear may be as attuned to the intricacies of natural music as the ear of a musicologist is to the complexities of Bach or Bartók.

The bird sounds are not necessarily beautiful, even to the most dedicated Auduboner. The harsh twanging of the Brewer's blackbird or the raucous

154

squawk of the jay can scarcely be called music, although they certainly have character. Even the song of the robbin would hardly win any prizes for melody. It is less a song than a long series of disconnected notes and phrases with brief pauses between, as if the bird were hesitantly experimenting but too shy and lacking in self-confidence really to rear back and belt out a tune. Someone has speculated that the robin is conceiving of intricate musical passages beyond the range of his voice and is able to reproduce only tantalizing fragments of the unheard melodies, like an amateur tenor who can manage only the middle notes of an elaborate aria.

Whatever the story behind the robin's diffident musical statement and however plain it may be compared to the more ornate songs of other birds, it has an appeal beyond the limited range of its notes. For it is the traditional herald of spring, and like a fragment of an old popular tune that may have little intrinsic merit but brings back a flood of recollections of other times and other places, the robin's song evokes images of the first green grass, the returning sun, the swelling buds, the season when the world is young and each morning is full of promise. For this writer one of the strongest sensations set off by the voice of a robin is a recollection of awakening on a May morning in Yosemite Valley and hearing the song while I peered out of a sleeping bag at the first rays of the sun on the great granite wall at Glacier Point. The American colonists coming to the lonely New World shore also had a nostalgic feeling about this bird. It reminded them of the original robin redbreast of England, and they called it a robin, even though it is much larger and less red than its Old World namesake. Its dark-gray back, wings, and head and yellow bill are complemented by a breast that is not so much red as a rich golden brown.

In San Francisco the numbers of robins have almost kept pace with the growth in the human population, and particularly with the spread of trees, shrubs, and lawns that provided food and shelter not available in the original dunes. At first robins came here only during the winter, retreating from harsher mountain climates for the season. But in the summer of 1915 an assiduous bird watcher was amazed to encounter a robin in Golden Gate Park—along with human visitors who had come for the World's Fair. Evidently the bird was a scout and found the park worms tasty, the berries succulent, and the trees suitable for housing. Over the years the numbers have steadily increased until there are now nearly as many in summer as

155

in winter. Apparently, however, the summer and winter populations are different. The wintering robins depart in the spring for the inland valleys and mountains and are replaced by summer birds moving in from the south. Nowadays an occasional robin song might be heard almost any time of the year, but the greatest volume of bird music of all kinds comes with the amorous impulses of spring.

Equally vocal and almost as numerous in the city's parks and yards are the sparrows, smaller than the robins and an inconspicuous gray. The white-crowned sparrow, distinguished by white stripes around the eye, has a song that begins with one long whistled note, a second equally long note on a higher key, then a trill on an intermediate key. The golden-crowned sparrow has an even more easily identifiable song—three descending notes that sound like an off-key rendition of "Three Blind Mice."

Feathered Artists

To this bird-listener's ear the most mellifluous of all bird songs normally heard in the city is the limpid call of the meadowlark, bringing recollections of dewy spring mornings, open fields, rolling hills, bright sun, and the first blues and golds of the early lupine and poppies. The meadowlark's voice has been described as flutelike, but no human instrument can match these pure crystal tones. They are joined in a song of seven to ten notes that are never quite the same from bird to bird. The meadowlark is an individualist among songsters, and you can learn to recognize each bird by his favorite call, although he may vary the arrangement from time to time. My own college education was conditioned, for better or for worse, by one meadowlark that was fond of giving his call from the top of the gabled roof of one of the university buildings in such a way that it entered the windows of dozens of classrooms and set students who were supposed to be conjugating French verbs to dreaming of the open road and the tall grass. The meadow-lark has become increasingly uncommon in San Francisco owing to his fondness for the vanishing grasslands and open spaces. One of the best locations to hear his music is the top of Twin Peaks early on a spring morning, where a call from a bird perched high in the radio antenna may be answered by two or three others on a rock or post on the chaparral-

1 5 6

covered slopes, a pastoral concerto accompanied by the surflike roar of the metropolis below.

More rarely heard in San Francisco is the supreme musical artist of the feathered world—and maybe of any world—the mockingbird. The English poet who wrote rhapsodies to the Old World skylarks and nightingales should have heard this bird. His is perhaps the song dreamed of by the robin but not even remotely attained except in wishful fragments. The mockingbird is slightly smaller than the robin, gray with a long upturned tail. His wings flash with white when he flies. He is not, as his name might indicate, a mere imitator. He is a musician who weaves into his compositions the common folk tunes of his race, with variations and elaborations and intricate thematic interweavings that give his work the mark of high art and hold the listener spellbound with his virtuosity. Although he may improvise on the same theme for some time, he never precisely repeats himself but pours out a torrent of melody with lusty exuberance that is seldom modulated and sometimes continues far into the night, often to the discomfiture of householders who are more interested in sleep than art at 2 A.M.

Until recent years the mockingbird was unknown in San Francisco. He prefers the less foggy, windy climates of the inland valleys and is abundant in the Bay Area wherever a range of hills gives shelter from the ocean, but he is beginning to be seen occasionally even within the city. One morning a number of years ago I was on a hill in the Presidio looking down on the bay and suddenly experienced a pang of recollection without knowing for a moment what caused it. It was a mockingbird, all right, perched on a shrub a hundred yards away, giving full melodic expression to the magnificence of the view below. More recently I heard the fabulous music in the high valley just east of Golden Gate Heights, but never over a period of weeks was I able to locate its source, which always seemed to be behind a house or around a corner.

A friend from the East once asked if I knew the identity of a bird he had seen hovering high in the air, beating its wings, then making a spectacular dive toward the earth. My first guess was a sparrow hawk, but soon afterward, in the same garden, I saw what may have been the same bird. It was much smaller than I had assumed, with a long bill, iridescent feathers, and wings that beat so rapidly they were well-nigh invisible—ob-

1 5 7

viously a hummingbird. The "hum" is not a vocal sound but the whirring of the wings as they stir the air into vibration and enable the bird to "sit" in mid-air or hover in front of a flower as his long bill dips in for honey. Then he will back out without touching a petal—the only bird in the world that can fly backward.

Bird experts can readily distinguish between the three hummingbird types seen here—the Anna, the Allen, and the rufous—not only by their markings but also by the different pitch of the sound made by their wings and their varying patterns of flight, which involve pendulous dippings and swayings as well as dives and climbs. The male hummingbird is quite a show-off and his springtime aerial acrobatics are performed primarily to impress the girl friend.

The Ducks and the Phoenix

Even a casual knowledge of birds can lend an extra dimension to the daily routine. For me it is always a special experience, while walking in the outer reaches of Golden Gate Park, to flush out a covey of California quail. Even though the big top-knotted bird is abundant in the park, the sudden whirring of wings in the brush and the distinctive three-note warning call always comes as a surprise and brings a recollection of the same experience on hikes in the foothills in the days before they were covered with subdivisions. Once, during a stroll in the Presidio near Mountain Lake, I heard a faint bird call that took me back to one spring in Washington, D.C. We lived at the edge of that splendid natural woodland known as Glover-Archbold Park, and it was there I first heard the haunting, unearthly song of the veery, a softly resonant downward spiral of double-toned notes that seemed to issue from the heart of the forest, the disembodied spirit of wildness. The bird in the Presidio was undoubtedly not a veery, which is not normally found in California, but probably a Swainson's thrush, another member of the same family, yet the resemblance was close enough to make me think for a moment that I was three thousand miles away in the woods in the refulgent Eastern spring.

One sunny afternoon I spotted a pair of big black ravens flying along the cliffs of the Golden Gate below the Presidio. Thanks to Edgar Allan Poe the bright day seemed to have a temporary darkness about it; the birds were as symbolic as the crows in a Van Gogh cornfield. An opposite kind of emotion was stirred one Sunday noon when I was near the Arboretum in Golden Gate Park, happened to look up to the treetops and saw there in the sky a sight I had encountered only once before: a flock of white pelicans soaring overhead. There are few flying birds on earth as large as these; they commonly have a nine-foot wingspread, and there is nothing to match the grace and majesty of their coordinated patterns of flight. When I first spotted this flock, thirty or so of the huge birds were flying in a long follow-the-leader file, each individual's turning, rising, and falling followed exactly by the bird behind him. Then they circled and began to wheel in big spirals for several moments before falling in line again and disappearing over the eucalyptus tops to the west.

With the exception of the Chain of Lakes in the west end of Golden Gate Park, most of the park's lakes are man-made, but the water birds flock to them as readily as if they had been provided by nature for that purpose. Of the ducks, the most numerous and familiar is the big mallard, recognizable by his green head and narrow white collar. He is on all the park's lakes the year round and will eat out of your hand if given the slightest encouragement. The only other duck numerous here all year round is the ruddy duck, a dark red bird with white cheeks, about half the size of the mallard. Unlike the mallard, who feeds on the surface, merely "ducking" his head occasionally, the ruddy is a diver and will disappear beneath the water for what seems minutes at a time. He refuses to come ashore, mainly because he never learned to walk on land, and even naps while floating, head under wing. The widgeon, not a diver but a "dabbling" duck like the mallard, is here only in the winter and heads in the spring for the nesting grounds, principally in the northerly inland areas from northeastern California to Alaska. He is recognizable chiefly by his white crown and mainly brown body. Also migrating to the inland north in the summer are the pintail, a dabbler, common in the winter at Stow Lake, identified by a long, pin-thin tail, and the canvasback, a diver, light-colored except for reddish head and neck, more abundant in the winter at Spreckels Lake.

The females of all these species are a drab color and more difficult to identify. The all-white duck seen around most of the lakes is an introduced hybrid, the Peking duck, which was originally bred in China for food purposes. How the white birds got into the park in such numbers

159

is anybody's guess. Probably many of them (or their forebears) were given to children as Easter ducklings, were kept around the house until they got too big for comfort and were released in the park.

Most San Franciscans are probably unaware of the fact that their city has an "official bird." Oddly enough, this bird, which is pictured on the city's flag, has never been seen in the city. It has, in fact, never been seen anywhere. It is the phoenix, a single bird of Egyptian mythology which is said to have lived for five hundred years in the Arabian desert and then, apparently fed up with old age, set itself afire and rose renewed from the ashes, young and beautiful. San Francisco had burned down and risen from the ashes several times before the holocaust of 1906 (young, perhaps, though hardly beautiful) and the symbol may be appropriate enough from a historical standpoint. But it would seem even more fitting to choose as the city's symbol not a nonexistent creature from musty legend, but a living bird that is more identified with the city than any other—the gull.

Birds of Pleasure

The big white birds that sail effortlessly over the city and the bay in totally admirable patterns of flight are as inseparable a part of the tone and texture of San Francisco as the bridges, the waterfront, the parks and the hills. In the old days the gulls followed the ferries, and commuters could identify individual birds that sometimes adopted a particular boat. They still follow the fishing boats, swarm over the water during the herring runs, perch by the hundred on the roofs of the Embarcadero wharves. As a civic symbol they would fit San Francisco's reputation as a fun-loving city. The flight of gulls often seems to be a matter of sheer pleasure, particularly on windy days when they catch the updrafts over Telegraph Hill or Twin Peaks or even downtown skyscrapers, soar and zoom and circle and dip and slide down the currents like youngsters at the Fun House.

They are early risers, and often just before dawn you can see them flying high, catching the first rays of the sun while the city is still in shadow, moving singly or in groups of four or five from their roosting places on the docks and the girders of the Bay Bridge, southeast over Mount Sutro and Twin Peaks, probably bound for Lake Merced for a fresh-water bath or breakfast on the beach. Another of their favorite corridors across the city is over Golden Gate Park, where they frequently stop off either for a lake swim or for a worm hunt on the park's bigger lawns. They congregate by the hundreds, particularly after a rain has brought the earthworms to the surface, on the Polo Field, nearby Speedway Meadow and along the shore of the bay at the Marina Green, setting up a chorus of mewings, cluckings, and chucklings that can be heard far and wide.

The most impressive gull sight of all is on winter evenings at sundown when the birds return from the ocean to their roosting places on the inner waterfront, flying in irregular groups and long ragged files. Thousands of them may pass overhead for an hour or more in a long procession, flight after flight moving eastward over the Presidio shore, the Marina, and Fort Mason. Visitors to Aquatic Park and Fisherman's Wharf gaze up at the spectacle, which often continues as the colors change in the sky, the sunset hues turn to gray, and the birds become barely distinguishable shadows in the gathering dark.

The flight patterns of gulls and other soaring birds have long been studied by scientists for clues as to the action of wind currents. For centuries men have been puzzled as to how the birds could remain aloft and even gain altitude without moving a wing. In a high wind, of course, the explanation is not so difficult. The horizontally moving air hits a hill or a cliff or a building and is deflected vertically in a continual jet on which the bird can float indefinitely. Soaring over the open ocean requires more ingenuity. Here the bird takes advantage of the fact that the wind moving immediately above the surface is slowed by friction with the water. If he is headed for the shore, he flies in the opposite direction, low on the water and into the wind. Then he uses his momentum to rise upward to a level where the wind is blowing faster, turns around and glides shoreward on the swifter velocities aloft. When he has lost altitude until he is again down near the surface in the slower-moving air currents, he turns back into the wind and repeats the performance, gaining distance—and saving energy during the glide—on each loop.

Even more arresting is the sight of a bird soaring upward on a day when there is no wind, gaining altitude without a wingbeat. Studying this phenomenon, scientists have discovered valuable data on movements of air, adding to their knowledge of meteorology. On a warm day the morning sun heats the ground unevenly; bare soil, for example, reflects more heat than

1 6 1

ground covered by foliage; and consequently the air over the bare ground gets hotter. Over this hot spot the heated air forms an air "bubble," much as a bubble is formed on the bottom of a pan of heated water. The air bubble boils upward, creating what plane pilots call a "thermal" and what passengers call "bumpy air." The bird rides a thermal as if it were an elevator and is lifted without effort.

Actually the motion of air within the thermal shell is highly complicated, requiring the bird to be an expert in air movements. The warm-air bubble evolves into the shape of a doughnut; cooler air circulates upward through the hole and downward around the periphery. The bird's job is to circle within the hole, finding the exact radius that takes advantage of the maximum updraft of the cooler air. The birds have known all about thermal shells for millenniums, but scientists knew very little about them until they discovered the structure by careful observation of soaring birds.

Gull Talk

Scientists observing the behavior of gulls have discovered that the birds have a language of their own, communicating by voice and gestures. Just as with human beings, the language differs from species to species but has certain basic resemblances. There are special food calls that attract other gulls and alarm calls to warn other members of the flock of danger. A "mewing" sound is made by parents to attract their young, and harshly defiant calls are given by males in breeding season to scare off other males. Conveniently, the same call attracts females.

Other signals are conveyed by posture. A gull rears into an upright position, head high with bill down and wings slightly raised, to indicate hostility, perhaps toward an intruder who has ventured into his territory. The gesture is comparable to fist-shaking in humans. And since gulls are practical animals and have few worries about saving face, the intruder confronted with such behavior will often turn his back, averting his bill, perhaps even tucking it under his wing, as a sign of appeasement, avoiding battle. If the upright posture does not repel the invader, a gull will still try to avoid a fight by other warning gestures. He may peck at the ground and tear up some grass to show the intruder what will happen to him if he doesn't retreat. If this elaborate charade does not succeed, a battle may yet ensue, but not until after efforts have been made to avoid a showdown. Perhaps rival nations indulging in brinksmanship could take a lesson from the gulls.

Among the most numerous of the eight species of gulls commonly seen around San Francisco, and the only species here the year round, is the big Western gull, identified by his black wings and back, white body and white head. Unlike the other species the Western does not leave for far breeding grounds in the spring but remains around the Bay Area, nesting at such locations as Point Reyes and the Farallones. But even those that nest on the islands often commute the twenty-five miles to the city and the bay daily for the businesslike activities involved in gaining a living. And they find no dearth of food, from the garbage dumps and sewage outlets to the seasonal runs of herring and smelt, and even the eggs and young of other species of birds. Clams are highly prized as food, but the hard shells of some species present a problem. Along the Atlantic coast some gulls have been observed carrying clams up to heights of twenty or thirty feet and dropping them on the rocks or pavement below to crack the shell. I have found no authenticated reports of local gulls using these tactics, possibly indicating either that the birds here are less resourceful or the bird watchers less observant.

About the same size as the Western gull and almost as numerous but much lighter in overall appearance is the glaucous-winged gull, a real blond, the only gull with no black plumage. In the spring this bird finds breeding and nesting grounds along the northern coast from Washington through British Columbia to Alaska and the Bering Sea. The immature gulls of this and most other species are a mottled brown or gray and more difficult to identify.

Smaller than these two species is the California gull, intermediate in coloring, with gray back and wings and greenish legs. Like the Western and glaucous-winged, this is one of the gulls that followed the ferries on San Francisco Bay, but the California gull also forages inland and may follow the plow of a farmer for the succulent worms turned up by the blade. This species is a prime example of the reason ornithologists object to the term "sea gull." None of the gulls is a sea bird in the same sense as are the albatross and other birds of the open ocean. At best they are coastal birds, although the California gull is scarcely even that; many move down to the coast for the winter but return in spring to the inland lakes. Mono Lake, on the far side of the Sierra two hundred miles east of San Francisco, is a

163

favorite breeding area for these birds, but they are found as far inland as Wyoming and North Dakota. Some never come near the ocean, wintering in the Great Basin area between the Sierra and the Rockies. It was probably the California gull that saved the crops of the Mormons at Salt Lake from the crickets a century ago, but we are unlikely ever to learn whether they flew all the way from California or were year-round inland residents.

Also common over the city are the ring-billed gull, smaller than the California gull, but otherwise similar except for the black ring near the tip of his bill; the mew gull, smaller yet, with a cry that gives him his name; the herring gull, one of the biggest, identified by his black wingtips and reddish legs; the Heermann's gull, easily distinguished by his overall dark gray color and red bill, restricted to salt water, going south in January to breed on Mexican islands; and the very small, black-headed Bonaparte's gull, named not for his diminutive size and aggressive manner but for Charles Lucien Jules Laurent Bonaparte, nephew of Napoleon I, who came to the United States in the 1820s (twenty-five years after his father Lucien had unsuccessfully tried to escape the Emperor's clutches by fleeing to this country), became interested in American birds, and wrote a four-volume treatise: *American Ornithology*.

When the Swallows Come Back . . .

Although the gull is the most traditionally San Franciscan of birds, there are birds in the city connected with traditions of other kinds. The swallows come back to San Francisco as regularly as to Capistrano, although the records here do not go back so far. Five species of swallows (out of seven found in California) arrive here every spring, and each species nests at a particular location in the vicinity of Lake Merced. Some also nest elsewhere in the city. They are not quite so punctual as the Capistrano swallows are reputed to be (neither, in fact, are the Capistrano swallows), but the cliff swallows usually begin to arrive in force between March 12 and 14 and, since buildings are more convenient than cliffs, construct their mud nests under the eaves and in protected locations at the zoo, at Fleishhacker Pool (where they nest under the diving platform) and at San Francisco State College. A few years ago when the swallow population seemed to be getting out of hand, the grounds keepers at the college tried to clean out their nests by hosing them down, incurring the wrath of the bird lovers, who feared that the young as well as the nests were being destroyed. The birds did quite well for themselves, however, and thwarted all efforts to drive them away, simply rebuilding the nests on nearby campus buildings.

Members of the biology department came to the rescue by suggesting more tactful methods of dealing with the birds. In locations where the nests would be particularly objectionable, over doors and walkways, the grounds staff strung up wires to discourage nesting and obligingly built plaster nests in unobjectionable locations, hoping the birds would move in. The cliff swallows evidently were delighted with the ready-made tract houses; they not only moved in but added their own mud embellishments and built additional nests next door. Everybody was happy with the results, including the Audubon Society.

Barn swallows, preferring indoor locations, find ample housing around the zoo, in the animal barns and enclosures, even in the lion compounds, where the earth-shaking roars of the great mammals evidently do not perturb the birds in the least. Zoo keepers are happy to have the birds arrive for the summer, as they feed on the insects that feed on the animals. In years when the barn swallows are abundant, the flies at the zoo are few.

Even more intriguing are the habits of the bank swallows, who prefer to build their nests in the earth. The banks and cliffs along the beach near Lake Merced are ideal, consisting principally of sand and soft earth where the digging is easy. These flocks arrive early in April, a few weeks later than the barn and cliff swallows. You can see them scouting the banks with their probing, darting flight that is so rapid your eye can scarcely keep up with it. They begin to work near the top of the cliff where it is steepest, and hover with invisibly rapid wingbeats while they scratch out a toehold with their feet. For several days the sand flies furiously. As the holes get deeper the birds disappear inside and nothing is visible but jets of sand spurting from the entrance. A swallow who may think he has found an old burrow to move into without the trouble of digging may well get an eyeful of sand from a bird who got there first.

When the hole has become a tunnel three or four feet deep, safe from the strongest blasts of the sea winds, the birds build their nests inside. The nest-building period is even more hectic; dozens of the quick darting birds fly in and out of adjacent tunnels simultaneously, bringing grass and other

1 6 5

nest materials, most of the time on what appears to be a collision course with their neighbors. How they avoid head-on fatalities in such swiftly moving traffic is a subject that might well repay study by the Civil Aeronautics Board.

. . . To Lake Merced

The swallows have been nesting in this general location for as long as the oldest bird watcher can remember, and their reasons for doing so throw light not only on their own habits but possibly on the evolution of the landscape itself. Colonies of bank swallows nest in many other locations along the coast, but this spot is unique. Elsewhere they colonize at the entrance to rivers or good-sized streams. One example is the mouth of the Russian River sixty miles to the north. The reason for the birds' fondness for fresh water is clear. They feed primarily on insects that breed in the water. They may prefer the coast for two reasons: the waves carve the kind of banks and cliffs that make ideal nesting grounds, and the coastline makes a naturally easy route to follow in their long migrations. Probably their original choice of location was made wherever in their coastwise flights they encountered the mouth of a river or stream, providing the essential fresh water. Here at Lake Merced, alone among the known coastal nesting sites, there is no stream flowing to the sea.

The lake in its natural state, however, did overflow into the ocean through a stream that found its way to the beach around the north end of a long sandspit. In the 1890s the stream was blocked off when the lake was dammed and its surface raised for reservoir purposes. It seems probable that the ancestors of these swallows began nesting here in the days when the water of the lake flowed into the ocean, some time before the 1890s. How much earlier the birds first arrived here is a matter open to speculation. It could even be argued that evolution of the lake indicates the birds have been coming here for hundreds or even thousands of years. The stream that flowed from Lake Merced into the ocean has never amounted to much in historic times, owing to the fact that only small streams flowed into the lake. Doubtless for a good portion of the year evaporation from the lake balanced inflow and there was no outflow into the ocean at all. This is exactly what happens at most mouths of small streams and lagoons along the coast, sealed off from the ocean by the flow of sand.

In the geologic past, however, when the lake was smaller or nonexistent, minimizing evaporation loss, it is likely that there was a much larger stream flowing to the sea. If it is assumed that the swallows would nest primarily only where a good-sized stream entered the ocean, they may well have chosen this location during a time of lower sea level when the stream flow here was substantial, more than a thousand years ago. If so, this swallow colony may be far older than that at Mission San Juan Capistrano, and we give permission for song-writers and legend-makers to make the most of it.

All this, of course, is piling assumption upon assumption in a highly unscientific manner. But it does no harm to speculate, and the theories are scarcely more improbable than the facts. It is a fact, for example, that the birds leave these cliffs every year near the end of August, within a few days of the same date. How do they know when the end of August arrives? Probably they perceive the southward movement of the sun and the increasing shortness of the days, but to gauge the date so closely reveals a better-than-human sensitivity science cannot yet explain. It is a fact, too, that the swallows follow the sun southward for thousands of miles, spend the winter in the warm tropical regions of South America, and set out again in the spring for the return trip at such a precise time as to arrive here every year very near the same date, regardless of wind, storms, or the leap-year vagaries of the human calendar. With their own inner calendars, the unknown mechanism that governs their arrivals and departures, their incredibly swift flight and ingenious ability to navigate and colonize, these birds symbolize the mystery and wonder of the wild creatures who are our fellow residents of this city on the peninsula.

167

Among the most conspicuous and numerous of the water birds in Golden Gate Park are the Peking ducks, here mingling with the familiar coots, or mudhens, on Middle Lake.

168

The Peking duck is a domesticated version of the mallard, ABOVE, a relationship visible in the similar profile and the curly tail feathers.

The widgeon, ABOVE, whose white crown gives him the alternate name of "baldpate," cruises along the shore of Stow Lake, and three shoveler ducks, BELOW, scoop up insects in their spoon-shaped bills as they paddle back and forth across Middle Lake like trawlers.

The most iridescently colorful of the duck family is the wood duck, who is fond of perching in trees and here at Middle Lake seems to have inspired a pair of mallards to do likewise.

Ruddy ducks and scaups enjoy salt water as well as fresh and go about their business in the bay no matter how thick the traffic.

172

During the winter herring runs, gulls swarm by the hundreds over the schools of fish, swooping and squawking in hungry excitement.

Many species of gulls cluster on the roofs of the Embarcadero wharves, enjoying the winter sunshine. The darker colored birds are principally immatures—two years old or younger. Perched on the rooftop, the gulls are as reliable indicators of the wind direction as weather vanes; they habitually face into the breeze in order that their feathers will be smoothed rather than ruffled.

1 7 4

The big Western gull is the only species that remains in the Bay Area all year round, while the others migrate northward or inland for the summer. Exceptions to this migration pattern are the Heermann's gulls, found more often along ocean beaches than around the bay. Dark-colored, with red bills, they stand here among the swash marks left by receding waves on an ebbing tide. They go south early in the year and breed only at one location—an island in the Gulf of California, returning in July and August.

Here, along a rocky beach below the Presidio, are clusters of big dark mussels and long goose-neck (stalked) barnacles. Acorn barnacles, shaped like miniature volcanoes, open to receive nourishment when the tide swirls around them. The barnacle is said to be an animal that stands on its head and kicks its food into its mouth with its foot, a description that is roughly correct. The mussels make good bait for amateur fishermen.

Clamped firmly to the rocks in the spray zone are smaller acorn barnacles, occasional snails, and numerous limpets, resembling small abalones. Here, at low tide when not even a dash of spray reaches them, the barnacles are closed tight.

ABOVE, hauled out of the deeps by professional fishermen are big Dungeness crabs, destined for the tables of Fisherman's Wharf. BELOW, a leopard shark stranded on the sand at Bakers Beach represents several species of relatively harmless sharks that cruise the waters around the city, cousins of the vicious man-eaters that occasionally attack swimmers and skin divers.

Alert strollers in Golden Gate Park can catch rare glimpses of wildlife in action, such as this hummingbird hovering in the fuchsia gardens, ready to plunge his bill into a flower for "honey."

179

Overhead in the Panhandle a flight of pigeons makes impressive patterns among the upper branches of the trees.

In the Japanese Tea Garden, ABOVE, Eastern gray squirrels play mercilessly on the heartstrings of visitors, begging food with the finesse of experienced panhandlers. The only squirrel native to San Francisco is the California ground squirrel, BELOW, who shuns the lush vegetation of the parks for the open dunes and fields and is pictured here among the mesembryanthemum carpets at Land's End.

Among the midget sandpipers that scoot rapidly along the low-tide flats in groups, following the edges of the waves in and out, probing the sand for succulent morsels, the most conspicuous are the sanderlings, distinguished from the others mainly by their light coloring and flashing wing stripes when in flight. Few wildlife phenomena are as fascinating to watch as the clockwork action of these delightful birds racing the advancing waves with legwork so fast it is almost invisible, apparently rolling across the flats like white billiard balls. The spectator is kept in breathless suspense wondering whether the minute birds will play the game of "brinksmanship" too closely and get caught by a wave. They never do.

At a distance the flight of these birds is deceptive. They
may bank in one direction, catching the sun, then turn
and become completely invisible until they bank again
in the opposite direction and appear as scintillating
flashes of sunlight. They are present along Ocean
Beach the year round except during the breeding months
of May and June, when they go as far north as the
islands of the Arctic.

183

The most familiar of the larger sandpipers that probe the flats with their long bills is the willet, a bird of the ocean's edge that feasts sumptuously on the sand crabs and other choice viands available just beneath the surface of the flat intertidal beach. Bubbles arising from the sand after a wave has receded are a sign to the willet that food may be available on the spot, and he makes haste to investigate. He may make several dozen probes for every one that is successful, but his persistence pays off. His thin legs offer little resistance to the rushing water, and he may wade up to the hocks, waiting for the wave to recede to resume his probing. In flight he displays distinctive white flashing wing stripes and may utter a loud screeching whistle that sounds like a cry of ultimate alarm. The white bird in flight near the two wading willets is a Bonaparte gull.

If you don't live near Sutro Forest, the Presidio, or Mount Davidson or prowl these wooded areas at night, you are unlikely to see the city's biggest and most audacious wild animal, the raccoon, who always looks as if he needs more sleep. But at the Junior Museum you might see a tame coon entertaining the youngsters (note the handlike paws), as well as a gray fox, and such non-natives as a kinkajou, an iguana, and a junior-sized alligator.

186

On a yellow mustard flower at the Presidio is that incredible migrant the Monarch butterfly, who travels hundreds and perhaps thousands of miles from mountain and inland areas possibly as distant as the Great Lakes to spend the winter in semidormant colonies clinging to the branches of trees in various groves along the California coast. Each flight arriving here in the fall is a new generation that has never before made the trip but follows precisely the migratory route of the previous generation, roosting in the same trees and navigating by some instinct still a mystery to science.

Biggest of the birds commonly seen around the city are the brown pelicans, with wing-spreads reaching six and a half feet. (The larger white pelicans are seen here rarely on their migrations.) They sail majestically through the air, often in formation, now and then giving a few flaps of the wings. Each bird takes his cue on flapping from the bird ahead in the formation. They often rest with other birds on Seal Rocks and spread their wings to dry. In flight not only do they resemble a squadron of big bombers, they actually engage in dive-bombing with great skill, plunging from the sky to hit the water with an enormous splash to snare a fish. Otherwise they are slow-moving birds, and often a quick gull can snatch a fish directly from their long ponderous bills. Occasionally a particularly daring gull will shadow a pelican on his daily rounds for this larcenous purpose.

188

The long-necked cormorants fly with rapid wingbeats just above the surface of the
water, sometimes singly or in small groups, sometimes in long files that may take half
an hour to pass a given point. They roost in large colonies at such bay sites as Red
Rock and Brooks Island and during the day head out for Seal Rocks and the stacks off
Land's End, where they dive for fish. They are able to remain under water for minutes
at a time, then they may perch on a rock digesting the meal and spreading their wings
to dry.

190

A soaring red-tailed hawk, based on Twin Peaks, rides the air currents a thousand feet above the city. Below, in the vertical hives of the downtown area, half a million people bend over their desks, oblivious to this symbol of wildness high overhead.

For a hundred years the roaring of the Steller sea lions on Seal Rocks served as a warning to navigators in the fog, but owing to the encroachments of civilization, the beefy mammals are seen and heard there less frequently these days.

A pigeon guillemot, a facile swimmer and diver and member of the auk family, rests on seamed sandstone at the foot of cliffs along the Golden Gate.

The northern phalarope is a long-distance flier, seen here at Lake Merced en route from the breeding grounds of the Arctic coast to spend the winter south of the equator. The phalarope has a peculiar habit of spinning on the water like a top, evidently to riffle the surface and turn up the insects, larvae, and plankton on which he feeds.

Part Five

THE SKY

The Great Procession

There is a day in spring when the fog returns like the triumphal homecoming of a Roman legion. It is heralded by the rhythmic trumpeting of the bass horns, echoing from the hills of the city early in the morning. The people listen and go to the heights to watch it arrive—to Telegraph Hill and to Twin Peaks, to the Presidio and to Vista Point on the Marin shore.

Its vapory banners glisten in the sun, and the sonorous music rises to a crescendo as it slowly advances, panoplied in light, on a mile-wide front through the Golden Gate. Hour by hour it pours through the strait in increasing volume, flowing under the deck of the bridge at first, then rising nearly to the tops of the towers. By mid-morning it may diminish and disappear before the increasing heat of the sun, but it will probably resume its march in the afternoon. Then, possibly on the evening of the second day, it lifts from the water into the air and becomes a canopy over the bay and its shores.

The advance of the summer fog over San Francisco Bay is surely one of earth's most impressive natural phenomena. To what other spectacle of nature can it be compared? Not to Niagara; it contains hundreds of Niagaras, all differing in size and shape. Not to the geysers of Yellowstone or the falls of Yosemite; its scale is far larger, its forms more varied. To the observant it is more than a spectacle. It is an experience of the senses. In the early stages of the cycle, when the fog is low in the streets of the city, you can feel its varied textures on your brow and its sea-freshness in your lungs. It is an experience of the spirit: it brings word of the elemental forces with which city dwellers too often lose touch—the turning of the earth, the flowing of the ocean waters, the rising of the giant winds. It is an experience of the imagination. It is as stimulating as great art or music to the observer who learns its basic form and rhythms, who can name its principal themes, who can trace perceptively its infinite variations.

The first advance announcements of the spectacle come in March or early April, when wreaths of vapor begin to collect over the beaches and coastal hills. The spring sun, moving north day by day, gradually warms the land. Over the inland valleys, the heated air rises, creating areas of low pressure, sucking cool sea air inland across the surface, causing the stiff spring breezes that blow from the ocean. The air masses, laden with invisible moisture from the sea, strike the coastal hills and rush up the slopes. As they rise they cool to the point at which some of their moisture condenses into visible vapor, forming wisps of fog and cloud that collect along the hills. From the western slopes of San Francisco, on many a spring day when the air overhead is clear, it is possible to see these small clouds forming on the seaward slopes of Mount Tamalpais to the north and over the sharp ridge of Montara Mountain to the south. As the sun declines and the air cools further, the vapor will form in the same way on the seaward slopes of the city's hills, then move with the wind eastward to the downtown districts.

Later in the spring and into summer the fogs will be formed by another process. When the wind blows through San Francisco en route to the warm Central Valley, it is not only sucked inland by valley heat but given an impetus from the rear by the Pacific High, a semipermanent high-pressure area of heavy, cool air sending out winds in various directions from its center in mid-ocean. Thus San Francisco's sea winds normally result from a combination of push and pull—a push from the Pacific High, a pull from the valley.

As the land grows hotter under the northward-moving spring sun, the ocean winds grow compensatingly stronger until they have a decisive effect on the surface of the waters beneath them. Drifting to the right because of the rotation of the earth, the winds hit the coast from the northwest and scuff along the surface of the coastal waters, creating a broad ocean current moving down the shore. The current itself is also deflected rightward by the earth's rotation and tends to flow away from the shoreline. To replace the waters drifting seaward, there comes an upwelling of cold waters from the ocean floor. Striking these cold upwelled waters, the moisture-laden masses of air from the ocean are themselves cooled until the water vapor in them condenses into visible form. Masses of fog begin to hang over the water and drift inland.

The exact birthplace of the fog may depend on the depth of the ocean. The continental shelf gradually slants down offshore, reaching depths of about three hundred feet near the Farallones, some twenty-five miles out. The water upwelled from these sunless depths is colder than the water rising from the shallower bottom near the shore. This difference of a few degrees in temperature may be enough to cause fog to form only over the colder offshore waters. On many a clear day in San Francisco it is possible to peer seaward from the city's heights and discern a massive bank of fog hanging off the coast near the Farallones.

Often as the air cools in late afternoon or evening, the bank will roll ponderously shoreward. It may not strike the land until long after dark or even early morning. Restive sleepers may hear, through the curtain of slumber, the reverberating voices of the horns in the bay and know then, half-consciously, that the city itself is wrapped in a thick white blanket of vapor.

Low and High, Wet and Dry

As the five-hundred-mile-long Central Valley heats up like an oven under the summer sun, the cool, foggy ocean air is drawn inward toward the valley through the only sea-level break in the valley's thousand-mile mountain perimeter, San Francisco Bay. For several successive days the fog and wind penetrate farther inland until the valley is cooled off. It ceases to draw the ocean air, and for the next few days the bay is fogless. But soon the sun heats the valley again, and the process is repeated. So develop the fog cycles which may last from three days to more than a week.

There is also a daily cycle: the fog begins to flow through the Gate in the afternoon, reaches a high point during the night, and burns off the next morning. And there is a seasonal cycle: as the season advances the fogs move inland more quickly, last longer, and tend to be higher in the air. They

196

reach a maximum during July and August, when the heat of the valley is most intense. But the best time to observe the forms of the fog is early spring or at the end of the season, in September and October, when it is most likely to come in low across the water and to develop the most distinctive variations.

The *fog front* may first be only a wispy finger of vapor drifting under the bridge. Eventually it will develop into a distinct wall several hundred feet high and as clearly defined as the advancing front of a glacier. Even ahead of the front there may be created *fog wreaths* at points where the incoming sea air strikes obstacles and rises above them. Air always cools as it rises, and the resulting condensation forms the wreath. The first wreath usually forms over Alcatraz Island, directly inside the Golden Gate. Another one often settles down on top of Angel Island. As the front advances, it often envelops Alcatraz in a *fog dome*. At first the dome may be translucent, and the island ironically seems surrounded by an aura. Later a much larger dome may form over Angel Island.

A *fog eddy* may develop along the edges of the Golden Gate, particularly at Kirby Cove just west of the bridge on the Marin shore. As the *fog roof* rises, the eddy in Kirby Cove mounts the ridge and pours over a cliff on the lee side—creating one of the area's many *fog falls*, which resemble nothing so much as slow-motion waterfalls. Here the falls strike the approach ramp of the bridge and the resulting mists drift through the bridge's harp-string cables like driven smoke. Wherever the front advances over the crest of a hill and moves down leeward slopes it creates a *fog cascade*. The most familiar and possibly the largest of these is the Twin Peaks cascade, visible on summer afternoons at the ends of Market and Mission streets. The entire east side of the mountain may be covered with a continuous smooth blanket of white vapor that rises and falls like an immense slow-motion surf.

This surf effect is particularly visible from the top of 2604-foot Mount Tamalpais north of the Golden Gate, where you can see the fog advance in waves or *fog surges*, with crests and troughs resembling those of swells on the ocean. At certain points the surges form surflike breakers or *fog combers*. Over Sausalito, for example, a comber several hundred feet high may hang suspended for hours, poised and ready to break. Just as rising air cools itself, so descending air grows warmer; as the forward part of the breaker descends, it evaporates into the warmer air. As a result, the wave seldom actually rolls down into Sausalito until the atmosphere cools after dark. One of the rarest of all fog phenomena is the *fog pyramid,* which seems to form inexplicably over such bodies of water as Richardson Bay in Marin, nearly as perfect in shape as the pyramid of Cheops and a hundred times as large.

Aside from these special fog forms, the summer fog is divided into two main types—low fog and high fog. The low fog is likely to be formed directly on the cold ocean surface and stays low as it moves inland. In San Francisco it flows thickly through the streets of Sunset and Richmond districts and moves ghostlike through the groves of outer Golden Gate Park. It envelops the deck of the Golden Gate Bridge, although the tops of the bridge towers rise above it into bright sunshine.

As the fog (known to weathermen as "stratus") moves across the Bay, it may stay low on the water and strike the eastern shore. More often, as it flows east it rises and moves to Berkeley at an elevation of several hundred feet, becoming high fog. But what is high fog in one location may be low fog in another. The fog bank that passes over downtown Berkeley will strike residential districts high in the hills, where it appears as low fog.

In San Francisco, after the stratus has been flowing in from the ocean for a day or two, it gradually rises and becomes high fog. The Golden Gate Bridge, which has been wrapped in vapors, becomes visible from the bottom upward, as if a curtain were rising. High fog, which may last for days (or occasionally for weeks in the areas near the ocean), appears as a general gray overcast, and summer tourists gloomily look for rain. But a Bay Area resident soon learns that no matter how dark the sky may be, rain in the summer is extremely unlikely. Visitors are often skeptical. "Why, then," they may ask, pointing out the window, "are the streets wet? What's that water all over everything?"

To answer properly, it is necessary to make a distinction between two further varieties of vapor—wet fog and dry fog. The wet fog, usually formed far out at sea, causes moisture to collect in big drops on trees, wires, eaves of houses, car windshields, and pavements. The dry fog, formed just offshore and composed of smaller drops, may seem equally impenetrable but does not produce a drip and no moisture collects, even on windshields. A drop in temperature, however, reducing the air's moisture-carrying capacity, can turn a dry fog into a wet one.

These two types of fog are very different in texture. Walk through either

198

kind and feel the difference on your face. The wet fog has a thick woolly consistency. Its large drops are coarse and granular. You can taste its salt on your lips and inhale its sea fragrance. But the texture of dry fog is smooth and silky. Although it may be as opaque as any wet fog, its consistency is thinner and more attenuated, like that of high mountain air. A wet fog is usually dark gray, even in the middle of the day. A dry fog, though brighter, may make vision even more difficult. It can contain great quantities of light, and its daytime brilliance may be painfully dazzling.

Often fog may be wet enough to create what amounts to rainfall in certain places, particularly under trees. In summers when the fogs are abnormally wet, the grass beneath coastal cypresses and eucalyptuses, which normally turns brown in late May, may be green through August. It is these wet fogs that produce the steady drip providing water for the redwood groves in coastal canyons during the long, rainless summers. The tall trees rarely grow naturally anywhere outside the range of the coastal summer fogs.

Aerial Spectacular

There are times when the fog moving across San Francisco Bay breaks all rules. Instead of a breeze through the Golden Gate, there come roaring winds that scuff the Bay into whitecaps, flail the branches of the eucalyptuses in the Presidio and Golden Gate Park, knock off the hats of tourists on Market Street and whip the flags of downtown buildings. Instead of a low mass of fog moving slowly across the surface of the bay, now there are flying banners and chunks and clouds of vapor that race in above the bridge and through the gaps in the coastal ridges every day for weeks at a time, colliding with skyscrapers on Nob Hill and Russian Hill, entangling the top of Coit Tower, throwing moving patterns of light and shade across the surface of the bay. Often the separate clouds will merge into a broken ceiling, then into a single layer of stratus, through which come gleams and shafts of sunlight.

This spectacular show of light and darkness takes place not only in the sky and on the bay but across the hills and valleys of the city. At one moment the valley of North Beach may be lost in gray shadow while the towered heights above it—Russian and Telegraph hills—shine in the sun. At the next moment the hilltops darken and the valley itself glows with light and color as the streets and parks and long rows of bay-windowed flats are thrown into sudden sharp relief. It is as if some ingenious stage manager at a hidden switchboard were experimenting with every possible combination of lighting effects across a stage consisting of the entire city and bay.

All day the translucent masses moving overhead are full of warm glowing lights, changing with the direction of the sun, from pearl gray to opal to blinding white. But once the sun disappears behind the western ridges, the play of lights across the sky changes abruptly. For a period of about forty-five minutes comes a strange interval that bears little resemblance to a conventional twilight. The fog, no longer illuminated by the sun, becomes black and foreboding against the pale light that remains in the sky. A bank of darkness hangs over the center of the bay, plants its foundations on the top of Angel Island, and extends across the dark water toward the eastern shore.

The sky's dying light glows around the edges of the dark strata and is reflected on the surface of the bay as in a black mirror. The lower edge of the blackness is a well-defined line against the luminescence of the water and the Marin shores. The dark bank extends skyward until its upper layers dissolve into separate wraiths of blackness that move eastward over the bay. Sometimes near Tamalpais there develops a rift in the strata and a sharp mass of light shoots down the mountainside at a forty-five-degree angle, setting ablaze a sector of Richardson Bay. For a moment it seems to slice the blackness like a bright sword, then suddenly it is absorbed into the enveloping dark.

Usually darkness is a void, a nothingness, a space without shape. But here, embodied in tangible vapors, it takes on form and substance. It is a positive force rather than a mere absence of light. And this is not only a darkness that has form; it is a darkness that moves. It is an animate thing, separating into indistinct shapes that expand and contract and dissolve and form again, all the while moving across the pale sky like a cloud of colossal bats flying across the interior of a dimly illuminated dome.

The interval is short. Soon the light fades and the dome itself darkens. The lights of the city begin to appear and are reflected against the lower layers of the moving fog, turning it into a misty luminous backdrop for the city's inner-lighted towers. Quickly the fog is drawn across the sky like a glowing canopy, and the darkness that a moment ago was embodied in the fog now resides in the waters of the bay. Yet it lacks there the quality of total foreboding blackness that was in the fog a few moments earlier. The darkness in the bay does not move; it has known limits; lights of ships and bridges are reflected on its surface. Over the neon of Fisherman's Wharf the flying masses of vapors are alight with misty reds and greens. Rolling over the eastern slope of Nob Hill, they reflect the garish yellow and orange signs of Chinatown. Above Market Street the harsh, bright lights of the theater district, sifted through the lower layers of fog, are transmuted into an opalescent glow.

The wind, no longer drawn forcefully into the interior by the daytime heat of the valleys, dies out into occasional gusts. After midnight, as the lights of the city begin to go out, the fog closes down. The fantastic flying shapes are gone, merging now into an amorphous mass that descends slowly, enveloping the towers on the hilltops. The thick white blanket lowers on the hills one by one, blots out the street lamps, presses down in the valleys with cool dampness, burying the sleeping city in swirling oceanic vapors.

Second Spring

Usually the realization that fall has arrived comes suddenly. It comes in a flash when you hear the thump of a punted football or the yells of the kids in a schoolyard that has been vacant all summer. Or you come out of the office after work and it's dark and you feel in your innards the cosmic fact that the sun has gone south and the long nights are beginning. In Golden Gate Park the elms slowly turn to yellow and the sycamores to brown. Along the roofs of the Embarcadero wharves the Western gulls are joined by the California gulls that have spent the summer on the inland lakes. The migrant ducks swarm to the lakes in the park and the odd-mannered phalarope whirls on the water, en route from the Arctic to the warm regions of the south.

As elsewhere, the most decisive sign of fall in San Francisco is a distinct change in the weather. In Miami the coming of the season is often heralded by hurricane winds, in Kansas City and Grand Rapids by dew on the grass; in Reno and Boise by early-morning frost in the fields. But San Francisco, as usual, goes by its own rules, quite the reverse of those in other parts of the country. Here the signs of the autumnal equinox are not wind, dew, or frost but increasing sunshine and rising temperatures. September and October are the two warmest months of the year. San Francisco's real summer is in the fall.

The Pacific High begins to move south with the sun, and its winds no longer reach this coast in force. The Central Valley grows cool during the long nights, and the slanting sun no longer heats it so intensely during the day. Gone are the ovenlike temperatures that sucked the cool sea air with its fogs in through the Golden Gate and over the city. The breezes, if any, are mild. In the parks, on the hills, and out over the bay there hangs the mellow haze of early autumn, like the nostalgic atmosphere in the painted landscapes of the French impressionists. These are the days when office workers crowd the squares of downtown San Francisco at noon, loaf for a few precious moments in the sun at Union Square or around the Mechanics Monument or in the park at the Crown-Zellerbach building, turn pale faces toward the light, hoping for a quick tan, and wander vaguely back toward the office a few minutes late. The foghorns may still send their threnody across the city, but the fog itself is confined to the ocean shores and the Golden Gate. Now, even more than in spring, the fog stays low on the water and flows like clinging vestments over the shapes of the land.

During the summer the Pacific High blocks the storms sweeping across the Pacific, deflecting them to Oregon, Washington, and British Columbia; but by October it usually has moved enough to allow the storms to hit the coast increasingly farther south. By November they usually begin to strike San Francisco sporadically. A few days of rain may be followed by a few days of sunshine. The result is another of San Francisco's meteorological peculiarities, a second spring. The ocean, which does not change much in temperature, acts as a thermostat, not only preventing summers being very hot but keeping the temperature up in fall and winter, considerably higher than the temperatures of the parts of the Bay Area separated from the ocean by hills.

In the city's vacant lots and hillsides, on uncultivated land in Golden Gate Park and the Presidio, above the cliffs at Land's End and on the rolling hills of McLaren Park, the brown grass of summer is replaced by the green of this second spring, and wildflowers begin to bloom—the fragrant sweet alyssum, the yellow spikes of goldenrod. Along the hilltops the bleached fuzz of *Baccharis*—coyote brush—catches and reflects the slanting light. Once again, as

202

in the spring, you can hear the call of the meadowlark, the hesitant chirp of the robin, the "three-blind-mice" melody of the golden-crowned sparrow, freshly arrived from the frosty mountains.

The city's second spring is as deceptive, however, as the false spring brought to the plains states by a chinook wind. A few warm days may be followed by a storm and, after the earth is damp, by the thick tule fog that develops in the cold tule marshes and inner valleys and flows slowly toward the ocean. It is properly called radiation fog; as the nights grow longer and colder the earth radiates or loses its heat upward, becomes increasingly cold, and cools by contact the lower layers of air. The moisture the air has absorbed from the rain-soaked earth begins to condense and develops into thick, low-lying vapor. Because air always tends to move from cold to warmer areas, the fog-laden air comes draining down through Carquinez Strait and spreads around the bay from the north, flowing outward through the Golden Gate to the ocean, reversing the direction of the summer fog. Sometimes the tule fog dissipates in the warmer temperatures near the ocean; sometimes the flow is copious enough to spread out along the coast. Often the oceanside Richmond and Sunset districts, known as the fog belt in summertime, remain warmed in winter by the sun while the downtown districts are buried in white layers hundreds of feet deep. Usually the tule fogs will remain until a new storm blows into the area and dissipates the vapors, but when the wind dies down after the storm the fog-forming process begins again.

The Winds of the City

The winds of San Francisco are of many kinds, and anyone with a sensitive nose can learn to predict the weather by sniffing the breeze and determining its direction. For some years we lived on Telegraph Hill and learned to anticipate the day's weather before getting out of bed in the morning. The aromas drifting in the window were sure signs of things to come. If the odor was salty, we could expect cool, breezy weather off the ocean and probably fog. But a pungent aroma from the coffee roasters near the Ferry building would be borne on a south wind, a reliable indication of an approaching rainstorm. An odor of burning or an acrid tang in the air meant the breeze was coming from the industrial areas northeast of the bay, particularly the oil refineries at Richmond and beyond. The day was sure to be sharp, clear, dry, and extraordinarily cold if the season was winter, or equally clear and dry but unusually warm at any other season.

From almost any point in the city, the same kinds of predictions can be made by anyone with a perceptive nose. Hilltops provide the clearest indication of wind direction. Elsewhere, particularly among high buildings, eddies and countercurrents may confuse the direction locally, although the odors will still be a reliable test.

The explanation for these odors on the wind arises from this region's distinctive meteorology. In any part of the earth, the rivers of air that move across land and sea from various directions bring with them distinct kinds of weather, but the weather-bearing winds of the Bay Area are unique in their variety and intensity. The reason is topography. As the only sea-level break in the Coast Range, the Golden Gate in particular and San Francisco Bay in general act as a funnel for the air masses that move between sea and land. There are three main types of winds that channel through this gap, each with its own temperature, humidity, general tone and flavor; and not only the visibility but the activities and dispositions of the residents are strongly influenced by the balance of forces in the atmosphere.

The salty sea breeze, blowing from the west in summer, whips through the Golden Gate as if the strait were a door left open, permitting a strong draft to blow from the cool outer regions to the warm interior. The south wind, heralding rain and bringing the smell of coffee to the northeastern part of the city, is part of a vast air mass that revolves counterclockwise for hundreds of miles around a storm center. Its precise direction is a clue to the kind of storm approaching. A wind from the southwest indicates a storm center moving in from the northwest, probably from the Gulf of Alaska region, bringing cold weather to the lowlands, snow to the mountains, and joy to the hearts of Sierra skiers. A southeasterly blow, however, indicates the approach of a southern storm, possibly from the Hawaiian area, boding ill for skiers. Its warmer air is capable of holding more moisture than the cold air of the northern storms. Owing to this larger water-carrying capacity, this is the kind of storm most likely to bring floods, particularly if it occurs at the time of a deep snow pack, which the warm rains will convert into slush and runoff, sending rampaging creeks into swollen rivers.

204

As the storm passes on eastward, the winds, continuing to revolve counter-clockwise about the vortex, hit the Bay Area from other directions. Check your windows. If your house is exposed directly to the winds, the south windows will be drenched during the early part of the storm while the other windows remain almost dry. Then, if the storm center is passing to the north, the wind direction will gradually shift until the west windows take the brunt of the attack. And, finally, if you see the north windows bespattered, you know that the storm center has passed on eastward and the rain is about over. With the cold air coming down from the north at the end of the storm, temperatures drop and there may be a couple of days of brisk, breezy weather.

Since the hardest rain usually falls during the early part of a storm, when the wind is southerly, the south sides of hills are likely to get more total rainfall than the other sides. The heaviest rain falls near the heads of south-facing canyons and valleys, where the south winds are trapped and forced to rise, cool, and lose their moisture. In San Francisco more rain can be expected to fall on the southern slopes of Twin Peaks and Mount Davidson, for example, than on the north.

The third kind of river of air moving into the Bay Area is the northeaster. This is a movement of continental air masses toward the ocean and brings the dry air of the Great Basin, the plateaus and high deserts between the Sierra Nevada and the Rockies, and sometimes arctic air siphoning south-ward from Canada. The moisture-filled marine air is pushed out over the ocean, and the invading dry air mass brings a unique clarity to the atmosphere, as if it were burnished like fine crystal. These are the days when all the shores of the bay are sharply defined, and the blue surface gleams in the sun for fifty miles. The dry continental air is further dried out and heated as it loses elevation. In a process the meteorologists call "adiabatic heating" the descending air warms up about five and a half degrees per thousand feet. Coming down from levels above seven thousand feet, the air may warm up forty degrees or more.

During the winter, however, a cold air mass from the Canadian plains may originally be close to zero in temperature and even though it rises forty degrees still strikes the Bay Area with frigid winds that send pedestrians to shivering in doorways and turning up coat collars. But in the spring or fall, the temperature of the continental air mass may be forty to fifty degrees, and a forty-degree rise will result in blasts of hot air that cause chapped lips and parched throats in San Francisco.

This is "fire weather," when humidity plummets toward zero and everything flammable turns to tinder, particularly dry grass and chaparral. The slightest spark sets off a blazing inferno propelled by the hot dry winds. The disastrous fires that occasionally strike the Bay Area have usually been fanned by northeasters. Although the 1906 fire came during an almost windless interval, the fire that leveled a large part of Berkeley in September 1923 and one that roared down on Mill Valley five years later were propelled by dry northeasters and raged unchecked until the winds blew themselves out and the normal moist ocean breezes returned to aid the firefighters.

Sometimes the dry continental air comes not as a wind but merely as a gentle movement of atmosphere that seeps down into the Bay Area, bringing warm clear weather and sending pale-faced San Franciscans again to the park and beaches. If it is February or March, the blossoms appear on the fruit trees, the acacias burst out in masses of fragrant yellow, hillsides are flecked with blue and gold of lupine and poppies, and you stare moodily out of the office or schoolroom window, dreaming, whatever your age, the dreams of youth and spring. But beware. Far out over the heaving blue surface of the North Pacific, in the conjunction of warm and cold air masses, there are probably brewing new storms and new winds.

The Meeting of the Seasons

There are times at the turn of the seasons when winter and summer phenomena occur simultaneously. I remember one Saturday night in the middle of March when it became evident that something momentous was taking place over the city. The afternoon had been unseasonably warm, but as we left the theater downtown that evening the temperature had dropped fifteen degrees and the air was damp and cold and salty.

We drove west and hit the incoming fog front at the Panhandle. This in itself was a major event. All winter the tule fogs had been moving down from the inland valleys toward the ocean, but here was the first of the summer fogs, flowing in from the Pacific even before winter had officially turned to spring. It came through the gap occupied by Golden Gate Park, and as we drove up the slope of the hill to the south we could look back down and see the vapor moving through the park in a long salient one hundred feet high. We were above it, and up here in the warm air inversion, the atmosphere was still balmy and dry and springlike. We could see the constellations glittering overhead and smell the aromas of blossoming fruit trees and acacias. During the rest of the night the sound of the horns at the Gate reverberated across the city—the double beep of the new Bonita horn, the sliding baritone-to-bass at Mile Rock, and the rhythmic antiphony of the three horns at the bridge.

Early Sunday morning it was obvious that something was out of gear. Besides the deep klaxons at the Gate, I could hear the horns in the inner bay—the banshee-contraltos on the Bay Bridge and the resonant diaphone at Yerba Buena, horns normally set off only by the tule fogs of winter. I got up about seven and headed for Twin Peaks to see if I could learn what was happening. The fog was thick overhead, and the streets were dark with rolling vapors. At about the six-hundred-foot level on Twin Peaks I suddenly emerged into bright sunshine that reflected so brilliantly from the roof of the fog that for a moment I was almost blinded. I continued to the top of the peaks, at nine hundred feet, and from there the fog extended out in all directions like a white, billowing sea. I was standing on a island, looking out across the dazzling surface to other islands rising into the clear upper atmosphere. To the west a mile or so was the crest of Golden Gate Heights, appearing like a long, low, tree-covered atoll, almost awash in a bright vapory ocean. Biggest of all the islands was the long ridge of Tamalpais to the north. The Douglas firs and live oaks of its upper slopes were clearly visible, glistening in the early sunlight. To the south was the nearby isle of eucalyptus-covered Mount Davidson, and several miles farther across the white surface was the humpbacked ridge of the San Bruno Mountains. Waves of vapor washed up on the slopes of the ridge and separated the main mass of the mountains from the foothills below.

Far on the southern horizon was one more island—Montara Ridge, from which Portolá's men first sighted San Francisco Bay in 1769. Now it seemed that the bay had risen six hundred feet and left no visible trace of life below. From where I stood the only signs of civilization were the TV towers of San Bruno, and they might have been remnants of some vanished culture, as anachronistic and mystifying as the ancient rocks of Stonehenge. The doleful sound of the foghorns came up through the vapors, as if mourning the passing of the drowned cities below.

I tried to dispel the illusion and determine what really had happened. Evidently this was one of those occasions that occur rarely at the turn of the seasons when there is a delicate equilibrium between the retiring forces of winter and the approaching forces of spring and summer. Yesterday, heated by the spring sun, the valleys had become sufficiently warm to begin to suck fog-bearing air in from the ocean. But during the night the inland areas had cooled off, and as usual during calm winter nights the tule fog had formed on the ground and drifted toward the warmer coastal regions.

In an encounter that happens perhaps only once in many years, the tule fogs from the land had come down to the bay and met the summer fogs from the ocean to form a continuous mass over the whole Bay Area. Winter was now confronting summer at this critical point of the year. The equilibrium between them could not last, and I waited to see which would win. Standing on this island I could feel the comfortable warmth of the sun on my back and watch the contest of forces like Xerxes on his hilltop at Salamis observing the Greek and Persian navies in deadly combat below.

Here in the warm air above the battle, the clear calls of the meadowlarks on the hilltop contrasted brilliantly with the muted chanting of the foghorns. The air was full of the smells of spring. The dew had left jewels on the hillside grass, and every blade shone with the colors of the spectrum. On the slopes of the peaks the first flowers, bedecked with the same crystalline gems, glowed in the early morning light—the pale purple of the lupine, the white of alyssum, the yellow of the mustard, and occasionally the bright gold of California poppies beginning to open in the warming sunshine.

The far-off sounds from below—the foghorns, the occasional bark of a dog or the tolling of a church bell—reminded me that millions of people were stirring in their beds or having breakfast, contemplating the dark vapors in the streets, totally unaware of this island of spring shining in the sun. To the east the accumulated tule fog seemed to be burning off, and below Twin Peaks I could occasionally glimpse vague patterns of streets and houses, as indistinct and distorted as if seen through swirling waters.

The first indication of the end of the deadlock between the aerial forces of winter and summer came when I detected a change in the odors. The scents of spring gave way to the smells of the sea, and I felt a sudden chill in the air. Looking west to the ridge of Golden Gate Heights, I could see that the tide was rising rapidly, and wave after wave of vapor swept over that island like the flood of a silent, slow-motion hurricane. Finally, after one particularly massive fog breaker, the treetops failed to reappear and the ridge was totally submerged.

The sun, heating the land areas, had set the air masses in motion, and all around the shores of the bay the warming air was rising, drawing the cooler sea air inland. Within about fifteen minutes the tide of sea fog rose in ponderous waves up the slopes of Twin Peaks until I was drenched and overwhelmed by the combers, and the entire island was inundated in a white flood that poured over the crest and flowed down the lee side in a colossal cascade. Summer had returned to San Francisco.

Late on a summer afternoon the great fog bank moves silently in from the ocean to engulf the low districts west of Twin Peaks and sends salients inward through the valleys, turning the western ridges into islands.

Over a period of two or three hours the white flood rises, pours over Twin Peaks, and flows down the eastern slopes like a cascade.

Sometimes, rather than flowing smoothly over the ridges, the fog comes like a giant raging ocean breaker, seen in slow motion, rising and falling as it plunges forward to engulf the city.

At other times it sifts slowly down through the buildings and trees of the eastern slopes like driven smoke.

After dark the fog closes in, and as seen from the Marin shore the city at night reposes under a smooth white blanket of vapor.

The lowest of low fogs, early in the cycle, ABOVE, moves in from the ocean under the Golden Gate Bridge, and motorists find themselves looking down on the fog roof. After perhaps an hour, the tide rises until the deck of the bridge is awash in the vapors and then inundated to a depth of about two hundred feet. Seen from the Presidio, BELOW, the flood piles up outside the bottleneck at the bridge and flows to a lower level over the bay.

Still the tide rises until only the tops of the bridge towers are visible.

At the Golden Gate the steel underwork of the bridge soars over old Fort Point, creating a shifting tracery of geometrical patterns.

215

As the mists lift from the water, ships are able to slide beneath the bridge with good visibility . . .

. . . and as the layer of vapor rises still higher the bay surface may be visible for miles beneath a ceiling of high fog.

Rising like a curtain, the fog layer reveals the Golden Gate Bridge from the bottom upward until the entire structure is visible under the overcast.

But a high fog to some may be a low fog to others. Seen from the Berkeley Hills, the fog deck canopies the bay, the Richmond-San Rafael Bridge, and the far shores.

The forms of the summer fog are infinite in number and change from year to year, day to day, and minute to minute. ABOVE, the vapor drifts through the Gate like puffs of smoke. Often it forms a halo or a dome over Angel Island, ABOVE RIGHT, or over Alcatraz, BELOW RIGHT, enveloping the abandoned prison in translucent vapors.

218

Sometimes the fog skips both islands and flows in a massive bank between them.

Finally, at the end of the fog cycle, when the solid mass breaks up into cumulus and then into misty wisps, the sun shines down through the broken ceiling, making dazzling patterns of light and shade on the face of the waters.

There are times in both summer and winter when the city is totally submerged in fog and only the mountain peaks around it rise above the white inundation like islands in the sun. Looking eastward from near the San Bruno Mountains on a winter morning only the Berkeley Hills and 3800-foot Mount Diablo are visible above the layers of tule fog, although at a point where the fog is thin, the shipyards of Hunters Point may be seen through the mists.

222

A wet fog, moving through a grove of trees such as these Monterey cypresses in the San Bruno range, will deposit substantial amounts of moisture on the leaves until they are thoroughly saturated and the water falls to the ground in a persistent precipitation called "fog drip." The same kind of fog produces a bejeweled effect on plants.

The low tule fogs of winter form over the land during the cold nights, sift through the canyons of the hills around the bay, move across the water and envelop the city from the east.

Reversing the pattern of the summer fogs, the tule fogs move outward toward the Golden Gate and the ocean. The Gate and the western districts may be clear while the downtown and eastern areas of the city are fogbound.

Through the thin blanket of tule fog, the light is vague and diffuse, creating misty patterns in the groves of eucalyptus and the pines and cypresses.

The winter fog clings to the lower elevations of the land, while the spires of the city sometimes rise above it.

227

Often the tule fog spreads a light veil over the waters of the bay.

228

Even after the main mass of fog burns off, thin mists may hang in the air throughout
the day.

The same mists may linger into the evening.

This is a city of winds that funnel through the Golden Gate and surrounding lowlands into the inner valleys of California as if a draft were blowing through an open door into a room.

231

The first signs of an approaching storm may come in late August or September while the summer fog still hangs over parts of the city—high wisps of mare's-tail cirrus, the outriders of a mass of warm humid air moving north from the Mexican gulf coasts.

The chances are the storm will not reach this far north, but if it does, the city can expect to see some of the thunder-shower type of rain that is rare in this region.

The second stage of an approaching storm front is a mass of high thin cirrostratus, ABOVE; like all cirrus clouds it consists of high-altitude particles of ice. This may be followed, BELOW, by cirrocumulus clouds lowering to altocumulus (the traditional mackerel sky or buttermilk sky).

The next stage might be the rain-bearing "nimbus" clouds such as these cumulonimbus over the Golden Gate.

Finally the low, dark nimbostratus clouds bring rain over the bay.

Intervals in the storm may permit sunlight to accentuate the shapes of the cumulo-nimbus clouds or create scenes such as this one over twin-spired Saint Ignatius Church, where one examines the clouds half expecting to discern the kind of winged hosts that appear in medieval paintings.

After the rain, the city is washed and clear, the air is cold . . .

. . . and the storm departs eastward with virtuoso displays of castellated cumulus.

239

Low bars of stratocumulus following the storm produce spectacular daybreaks . . .

240

. . . and sunsets.

EPILOGUE

Each wave, rolling in from some far storm, breaks with an impact that seems to shake the sand under your feet, rising high on the beach and receding to collide with the following wave in geysers of spray. The storm surf has shaped the beach at the water's edge into cusps—mounded points separating shallow embayments—and you can see the rising and falling patterns of sand extending rhythmically into the misty distance. Winter vapors roll through the air, and above the roar of the waves you hear the somber chorus of the foghorns.

Only vague traces of the Marin hills are visible across the water, and low in the southwest sky you can catch occasional glimpses of a pale disk of sun, reaching now at the winter solstice its southern limit, about to begin moving imperceptibly northward each day on its long journey toward summer. This is the time recognized by primitive man as the commencement of a new cycle of life, an occasion for rejoicing at the beginning of the sun's return; and modern man still celebrates his most significant festivals at this crucial moment of the year.

From out across the water you can hear bass whistles at intervals and discern in the vapors the silhouettes of passing freighters, many of them doubtless outbound with food and weapons and ammunition for the armed forces around this ocean. As you watch the ghostly procession, it occurs to you that three times within your adult lifetime ships have headed out this strait with troops and supplies for wars out there, where young men were dying because old men had failed to keep the peace. And now the threat of unimaginable holocaust arises out of a confrontation with the giant nation on the far shores of this sea. And you wonder, as you walk along the beach in the gloom of the dying year, if what you are doing day by day makes any sense in this kind of world.

A big wave deposits on the sand in front of you a large jellyfish, a crystalline mass of protoplasm, and you poke at it curiously for a moment before another wave carries it back into the surf. The tide is at the flood, and you hike higher along the sand, among the sea-sculptured driftwood and ribbons of kelp.

At the end of the broad beach you reach a rocky shoreline of cliffs and coves where the breakers are cutting small escarpments in the sand, carving miniature gorges, carrying away with each rush of water some of the sand that had been piled up there by the gentler waves of summer and fall. The waves are carving the rocks, too, over an imponderably longer time span, creating cracks and hollows and small caverns, and you climb over sharp-edged boulders that seem to have fallen only recently from the undermined cliffs above. In a stretch of a few hundred yards among the cliffs and boulders and outcrops you find a variety of rocks—walls of fossil-bearing chert in inch-thick, dark-red layers; smooth, hard sandstone surfaces; intrusions of soft serpentine as green as jade.

On the rocks at the water's edge is an amazing proliferation of life, mussels and barnacles and limpets clinging to the smooth walls, welcoming each successive wave as a bearer of food. You notice some limpets—small mollusks like button-sized abalones—clamped to the rocks not only at the water's edge but fifteen to twenty feet above, far from the reach of the waves. Yet these animals depend on the salt water for their food and apparently are prospering on the nourishment brought by the few drops of spray that occasionally reach them.

Above the cliffs, the mosses and lichens of the spray zone give way to the shoreline grasses and plants in profusion, occupying every inch of soil. And it occurs to you that life here is continually moving out, filling every available cranny, exploring every possibility, living in impossible places by impossible means of adaptation. Over the eons, the primitive plants and animals at the level of the kelp and the jellyfish and the barnacles developed through complicated proliferations into higher complex forms to fit every environment, to take advantage of every conceivable opportunity.

There were, of course, forms of life that failed. The vanished reptiles symbolize all the species that were unable to adapt to new circumstances and perished in one of evolution's dead ends. The Tyrannosaurus, for all his earth-shaking power, was far less adaptable than the primitive limpet and failed to make the transition from one kind of environment to another.

The bellow of a freighter comes from somewhere out in the fog, and it seems, as you walk along the ocean's edge at the turn of the year, that our own predicament is similar to the kind that at various times has confronted every species on this shore. Our environment is changing drastically. The old adaptations are outmoded; the old formulas no longer work. And the failure to adapt is summed up in the conflict on the far side of this ocean. It seems clear that the conflict and the failures that it symbolizes will never yield to conventional solutions but require new ways of thinking, new attitudes, new approaches not comprehensible within the tired formulas that belong to a bygone age. Maybe it is time for the kind of leap made by the limpet that first moved up to the new environment high on the rocks.

You find yourself wishing that all the decision-makers in the capitals of the nations could leave their offices and papers and telephones for a time, could confront the world outside the human hive, could see the total context in which human society is but one of many communities. Perhaps the richness and variety of the natural world, its profusion of forms and directions, its perennial exploration of possibilities, would evoke a corresponding richness of thought, an awareness of the broad ranges of opportunity beyond the confines of convention. Bemused by the hive, man finds himself in dead-end dilemmas that may have no exit except through the outer world where he can confront the elements of existence and develop a lively sense of new possibilities and new dimensions.

The sun has long since disappeared into the fog, and the light is rapidly fading. Racing an oncoming wave, you round a rocky point, reach a small beach, and at that moment confront a revelation. There, among mists that have momentarily parted like a curtain, is the colossus of the Gate, its arching deck pinpointed with amber lights, its webbed cables and twin towers soaring into the vaulted darkness.

It rises from the water's edge like an extension of these primeval rocks, a culmination of the earth forces that are shaping these cliffs and have produced the profusion of life on this shore. It is not a bridge, a fixed object joining shore to shore, but a direction, an affirmation, a leap forward, a thrust into the unknown, a stage in some further evolution leading to an unknowable future.

You stand there gazing until a wave washes high at your feet, reminding you that the tide is still rising, and the hour is late. You scramble back along the upper rocks at the foot of the cliff, just out of reach of the thundering combers.

INDEX

Alamo Square, 47
Alcatraz Island, 197, 218–20
Aldea San Miguel (Sutro Forest), 135
Alemany Gap, 20
American Ornothology (Bonaparte), 164
Angel Island, 200, 218–20
Animals. *See* Wildlife
Anza Vista, 47
Aquatic Park, 119, 161
Arguello lookout point, 47

Bakers Beach, 37, 45, 50, 51, 61, 67, 72
  changes in landscape on, 76
  mesembryanthemum on, 109
Bancroft, Hubert Howe, 121
Bareta, Angelo, 113
Baum, L. Frank, 139
Bay Area, 119, 137, 157, 160, 163, 175, 194, 196, 199–201, 202, 204, 205, 206
Bay Bridge, 34, 118, 207
Birds
  Allen hummingbirds, 158

Anna hummingbirds, 158
bank swallows, 165, 166–67
barn swallows, 165
blackbirds, 154
Bonaparte gulls, 164, 185
brown pelicans, 188
California gulls, 163, 164, 201
California quail, 158
canvasback ducks, 159
Capistrano swallows, 164
cliff swallows, 164, 165
coots, 168
cormorants, 190
doves, 149
ducks, 201
  all-white, 159–60, 168, 169
  canvasback, 159
  mallard, 159, 171
  Peking, 159–60, 168, 169
  pintail, 159
  ruddy, 159, 172
  widgeon, 159, 170
  wood, 171
flickers, red-shafted, 149
glaucous-winged gulls, 163

golden-crowned sparrows, 156, 203
guillemots, pigeon, 193
gulls, 160–64, 173, 174
  Bonaparte, 164, 185
  California, 163, 164, 201
  glaucous-winged, 163
  Heermann's, 164, 175
  herring, 164
  language of, 162–64
  new, 164
  ring-billed, 164
  Western, 163, 175, 201
hawks, red-tailed, 149, 191
Heermann's gulls, 164, 175
herring gulls, 164
hummingbirds, 179
  Allen, 158
  Anna, 158
  rufous, 158
jays, 155
juncos, 150
mallard ducks, 159, 171
meadowlarks, 156–57, 203
mockingbirds, 157
mudhens, 168

249

nightingales, 157
Peking ducks, 159–60, 168, 169
pelicans
  brown, 188
  white, 188
phalaropes, 193, 201
pigeon guillemots, 193
pigeons, 180
pintail ducks, 159
quail, 149
  California, 158
ravens, 158
red-shafted flickers, 149
red-tailed hawks, 149, 191
ring-billed gulls, 164
robins, 150, 155–56, 157, 203
ruddy ducks, 159, 172
rufous hummingbirds, 158
sandpipers, 182–85
skylarks, 157
sparrows
  golden-crowned, 156, 203
  white-crowned, 149, 156
Swainson's thrush, 158
swallows
  bank, 165, 166–67
  barn, 165
  Capistrano, 164
  cliff, 164, 165
thrush, Swainson's, 158
veery, 158
Western gulls, 163, 175, 201
white-crowned sparrows, 149, 156
white ducks, 188
widgeon ducks, 159, 170
willets, 185
wood ducks, 171
woodpeckers, 149
See also Wildlife
Bolinas, 39, 50

Bonaparte, Charles Lucien Jules Laurent, 164
Bonilla, Manuel G., 28–29
Brannan, Samuel, 119, 128
Brooks Island, 190
Brydon, P. H. "Jock," 146
Buena Vista Peak, 33, 123

California, University of, 119
  blue gum trees near, 87
  Extension campus, 46
  Hydraulic Engineering Laboratory, 40
  Medical Center, 98, 135
Carquinez, strait of, 40, 41, 203
Chain of Lakes (Golden Gate Park), 49, 100, 122, 142, 159
Chamisso, Adelbert von, 97
Children's Quarter (Golden Gate Park), 127
"China Beach." See Phelan Beach
Chinatown, 201
City Hall, 34
  and City Hall Gang, 123–24
  construction of, 123–24
  destroyed by earthquake of 1906, 123
Clark, William Squire, 70
Clark's Point, 70
Cliff House, 34, 37, 43, 64, 74, 75, 129, 136, 138, 139
  See also Golden Gate Park
Climate
  air masses
    continental, temperature of, 206
    effect on fog of, 195–96
  autumnal equinox, 201, 202
  chinook winds, 203

clouds (see main entry)
equinox, autumnal, 201, 202
fall, signs of, 201
"fire weather," 206
fog (see main entry)
meeting of the seasons, 206–9
mists, 229, 230
northeaster winds, 205
Pacific High, 202
rains (see winds)
seasons, meeting of the, 206–9
sea winds, 195, 204, 205
second spring, 201–3
south winds, 204
storm centers, 204–5
storms, 37–38, 77, 204–5, 232, 233, 234, 237
tule marshes, 203
winds, 203–6, 231
  chinook, 203
  northeasters, 205
  sea, 195, 204, 205
  south, 204
  storm, 37–38, 77, 204–5, 232, 233, 234
  three main types of, 204–5
  winter, 205
Clouds
  altocumulus, 234
  buttermilk sky, 234
  cirrocumulus, 234
  cirrostratus, 234
  cirrus, 234
    mare's-tail, 232
  cumulonimbus, 235, 237
  cumulus, castellated, 239
  mackerel sky, 234
  mare's-tail cirrus, 232
  nimbostratus, 236
  nimbus, 235
  stratocumulus, 240
  See also Climate

Coast Range, 20, 27, 31, 41, 50, 51, 99, 204
Coit Tower, 199
Colma sand formation, 61
Comstock Hotel, 56
Conservatory (Golden Gate Park), 88, 90, 106, 124
Conservatory Ridge (Golden Gate Park), 99
Corona Heights, 31, 56
Cow Hollow area, 49
Cow Palace, 28
Crown-Zellerbach building, 202

Davidson, Mount, 28, 31, 32, 33, 84, 88, 135, 137, 186, 207
Deep Lagoon. *See* Laguna Honda reservoir
De Laveaga Dell (Golden Gate Park), 144
De Young, Mike H. *See* Young, Mike H. de
Diablo, Mount, 222
Diamond Heights, 55
Drake's Bay, 39

Earthquake of 1906, 27, 123
El Polin. *See under* Presidio, the
Embarcadero wharves, 160, 174, 201
See also Fisherman's Wharf
Eschscholtz, Johann Friedrich, 97

Farallon Islands, 20, 21, 27, 40, 92, 153, 163, 196
Ferry building, 203
Fewer, Brian, 88
Fireman's Fund building, 47, 95
Fisherman's Wharf, 161, 178, 201

Fleishhacker Pool, 81, 164
Fleishhacker Zoo, 18
Flowers and plants
acacia blossoms, 89–93
agave, 112
alyssum, sweet, 56, 110, 149
Artemisia, 97
asters, sea, 136
azaleas, 147
Baccharis, 97
beach grass, 148
blue beach lupine, 97
California poppies, 96–97, 136, 149, 208
Ceanothus thyrsiflorus, 97
century plant, 112
chain fern, 146
coffee berry, 97
coyote brush, 97
cyclamens, 147
Eschscholzia californica, 97
fern, chain 146
forget-me-nots, 147
goldenrod, 149
hare's-tail grass, 111
heather, purple, 89
"Hottentot fig," 109
"ice plant," 136
Indian paintbrush, 136, 149
laurels, 98
lilac, wild, 97
lupines, 97, 136, 148
blue beach, 97
yellow beach, 97, 111, 149
Lupinus arboreus, 97
marguerites, white, 114
mesembryanthemum, 109, 136
poppies, California, 96–97, 136, 149, 208
purple heather, 89
redwood sorrel, 146
Rhamnus californica, 97
rhododendrons, 130, 147
sagebrush, 97

sand verbena, 136
sea asters, 136
sorrel, redwood, 146
Spanish broom, 110
sweet alyssum, 56, 110, 149
verbena, sand, 136
white marguerites, 114
wild lilac, 97
Woodwardia, 146
yellow beach lupine, 97, 111, 149
yellow mustard, 187
yerba buena, 96
Fog
birthplace of, 196
cascade, 197
combers, 197, 247
dome, 197
"drip," 223
dry, 198–99
eddy, 197
flying shapes of, 199–201
and fog horns, 207–8
front, 197
high, 198
low, 198, 214
marching, 42, 194–96, 199, 210, 211, 212, 213
and mists, 229, 230
pyramid, 198
radiation, 203
roof, 197, 214
seasonal cycles of, 196–97
shapes of, 218
spring, 197
summer, 194–95, 197, 199, 225, 232
surges, 197
tule, 203, 225, 226, 228
wet, 198–99, 223
winter, 225, 227 (*see also* tule)
wreaths, 197
See also Climate
Font, Father Pedro, 43, 49, 50, 96, 98, 142

Forest Hill district, 135
Fort Funston, 58, 61, 68, 80
  State Park, 135–36
Fort Mason, 87, 161
Fort Point. *See* Hunters Point-Fort Point Fault
Franciscan formation. *See under* Rocks
Frank H. Buck (tanker), 37, 66
Fraser, Hugh, 132–33
Fraser, Mrs. Hugh, 132–33
Funston, Frederick, 136
  See also Fort Funston

Garden of Fragrance for the Blind (Golden Gate Park), 96
Glen Canyon, 55
Golden Gate Bridge, 45, 63, 97, 118, 203, 207
  fogs at, 198, 214, 215–17
Golden Gate Heights, 31, 33, 48, 49, 53, 56, 59, 62, 97, 149, 157, 207, 209
  mesembryanthemum in, 109
Golden Gate Park, 14, 31, 33, 34, 35, 58, 137, 150, 202
  acacia trees in, 89–90, 122
  Chain of Lakes, 49, 100, 122, 142, 159
  Children's Quarter, 127
  Conservatory, 88, 90, 106, 124
  Conservatory Ridge, 99
  created by Hall, 120–23
  De Laveaga Dell, 144
  early financial problems with, 125

early political problems with, 123–27
  fogs in, 198, 206–7
  Garden of Fragrance for the Blind, 96
  Hall of Flowers, 90
  history of, 118–19
  Japanese Tea Garden, 130–33, 146, 152, 181
  John McLaren Memorial Rhododendron Dell, 130, 147
  Kezar Stadium, 127, 128
  McLaren Dell, 130, 147
  McLaren Lodge, 94, 104
  Main Drive, 88, 90, 124
  Marina Green, 161
  Middle Lake, 168, 170, 171
  Midwinter Fair of 1894, 126, 130–31
  Monterey cypress in, 94, 104, 122
  Monterey pines in, 106, 122
  Moon Bridge (*see* Japanese Tea Garden)
  Music Concourse, 116
  oak trees in, 98–99, 117
  Panhandle, 84, 87, 101, 106, 116, 122, 180, 206
    Freeway, proposed, 94
  Polo Field, 161
  Quarry Lake, 31, 34, 54, 145
  redwoods in, 98
  Sharon's Cottage, 127
  South Drive, 90
  Speedway Meadow, 128, 141, 161
  Stow Lake, 31, 120, 126, 127, 159, 170
  Strybing Arboretum, 96, 146, 159
  trees in, 82, 84, 148, 201
    eucalyptus trees in,

82–89, 101, 102, 122, 199
  West Speedway Meadow, 128, 141
  wild life in, 150–52, 154, 155, 158, 159, 161, 168, 170, 171, 179, 180, 181
Gold Rush times, 34, 49, 84, 90, 119
Great Bar, 38–41
  Ice-Age theory of, 40–41
  Main Channel entrance, 38–39, 41
  theories for existence of, 39–40
Great Sand Waste, 58
Green, George, Jr., 84

Hagiwara, George, 132, 133
Hagiwara, Goro, 132
Hagiwara, Makoto, 131–32
Hagiwara family, 132, 133
Hall, William Hammond, 35, 58, 83–84, 90, 94, 99, 117, 127, 128, 130, 142
  and creation of Golden Gate Park, 120–23
  political opposition to, 123–27
Hall of Flowers (Golden Gate Park), 90
Havens, Frank, 85
Hayes Valley district, 34, 50
Helmet Rock, 81
Howell, John Thomas, 96
Hudson, Roy, 129–30, 147
Huntington Falls, 126
Hunters Point, 28, 46, 222
Hunters Point-Fort Point Fault, 29, 63, 215
  belt of serpentine at, 45–46, 47

Hydraulic Engineering Laboratory (University of California), 40

"Island, The." *See* Strawberry Hill

James Lick Freeway, 46
Japanese Tea Garden (Golden Gate Park), 130–33, 146, 152, 181
John McLaren Memorial Rhododendron Dell (Golden Gate Park), 130, 147
Julius Kahn Playground, 95
Junior Museum, 31, 186

Kezar Stadium (Golden Gate Park), 127, 128
Kirby Cove, 197

Laguna de los Dolores, 50
Laguna Honda (Deep Lagoon) reservoir, 48–50, 135
Land's End, 36, 64, 65, 66, 68, 78, 97, 150, 151, 181, 190, 202
Laurel Hill, 47
Cemetery, 95, 113
Lawson, Andrew, 47
Lincoln Park, 36, 95
Linnaeus, Carolus, 15
Lobos Creek, 37, 61, 76, 98
oak trees at, 98
Lockridge, Ross, 91
Lone Mountain, 47, 98
Lyman Stewart (tanker), 37, 66

McCoppin, Frank, 119
McLaren, John, 35, 58, 84, 88, 90, 94, 98,

125, 131, 132, 146, 147, 148
Memorial Rhododendron Dell, 130, 147
as Superintendent of Golden Gate Park, 127–30
McLaren Dell (Golden Gate Park), 130, 147
McLaren Lodge (Golden Gate Park), 94, 104
McLaren Park, 28, 151, 202
Marina Green (Golden Gate Park), 161
Marin shore, 194, 200, 213, 244
Richardson Bay, 198, 200
Market Street district, 34, 46, 50, 97, 199, 201
Mark Hopkins Hotel, 56
Marsh, George Turner, 130
Marshall, James, 84
Mechanics Monument, 202
Menzies, Archibald, 97–98
Merced formation. *See under* Rocks
Merced Lake, 49, 80, 137, 160, 164, 165, 166–67, 193
oak trees around, 98
Merced Valley, 137
Middle Lake (Golden Gate Park), 168, 170, 171
Midwinter Fair of 1894 (Golden Gate Park), 126, 130–31
Mile Rock, 66, 81
Miller, Joaquin, 134
Mission district, 33, 46, 120, 122
Mission Dolores, 34, 50, 98
Montara Ridge, 207

Moon Bridge. *See* Golden Gate Park: Japanese Tea Garden
Moore, D. B., 41
Mountain Lake, 49, 96, 142
Music Concourse (Golden Gate Park), 116
Mussel Rock, 20
fossil cones found at, 92

Napoleon I, Emperor, 164
Needle Cove, 140
Newsom, Samuel, 132, 133
Nob Hill, 32, 56, 117, 199, 201
scrub oaks on, 98
North Beach, 199

Ocean Beach, 34, 36, 37, 39, 41, 42, 43, 53, 62, 136, 138, 183
Ocean margins, 34–37
low tide, 67, 68, 70, 80
storm waves, 37–38, 77
Ohioan (freighter), 140
Olmsted, Frederick Law, Jr., 88
Olmsted, Frederick Law, Sr., 96, 119, 122–23, 125, 127

Pacific Heights, 49, 98
Palace Hotel, 34, 124, 130
Panhandle (Golden Gate Park), 84, 87, 101, 106, 116, 122, 180, 206
Parks, 118–49
Aquatic Park, 119, 161
Fort Funston State Park, 135–36
Golden Gate Park (*see* main entry)
Lincoln Park, 36, 95
McLaren Park, 28, 151, 202

Ocean Beach (*see* main entry)
See also Presidio, the; Sutro Forest
Parnassus, Mount. *See* Sutro, Mount
Peattie, Donald Culross, 94
Phelan Beach, 71
Pine Lake, 49
Plants. *See* Flowers and Plants
Poe, Edgar Allan, 158
Point Bonita, 38, 43, 67
Point Lobos, 43, 97
Point Reyes Peninsula, 27, 163
Polk Gulch, 34, 117
Potato Patch, 38
Potrero Hill, 46
Prayerbook Cross, 31, 34
President Coolidge (liner), 66
Presidio, the, 36, 47, 79, 81, 97, 120, 136, 150, 151, 152, 154, 157, 158, 161, 176, 186, 187, 194, 202, 214
  El Polin, 143
  eucalyptus trees in, 82, 113, 199
  Heights, 95
  Monterey cypress in, 105
  Monterey pines in, 95
  oak trees in, 98
  parade ground at, 113
  sand beach on, 50–51
  wild lilac in, 97
  yellow lupine in, 111

Quarry Lake area, 31, 34, 54, 145
  See also Golden Gate Park

Radbruch, Dorothy, 28
Raintree County (Lockridge), 91

Ralston, William Chapman, 124, 127, 128
Red Rock, 190
Rhodes, Cecil, 126
Richardson Bay, 198, 200
Richmond district, 33, 34, 58, 89, 115, 136
  as fog belt, 203
  oil refineries at, 204
Richmond-San Rafael Bridge, 217
Rincon Hill, 34
Rocks
  bedrock, 30, 31, 57, 78, 79
  chert, 30, 31, 46, 53, 55, 56, 57, 62, 149, 245
  Colma formation, 80
  dipping beds, 31–33
  dunes, moving, 33–34
  earth blocks, 26–29, 30–33
  and faults in earth blocks, 26–29, 30–31, 57
  Franciscan chert, 62
  Franciscan formation, 26–27, 61, 137
  greenstone, volcanic, 56
  lava, molten, 31
  Merced formation, 61, 80, 137
  metamorphic, 81
  movements of major earth blocks, 27–29
  moving dunes, 33–34
  quartz, 79, 81
  river of sand, 34–35
  sandstone, 30, 31, 57, 73, 78, 79, 193
  serpentine, 81, 245
  serpentine belt, 45–47
  shale, 31, 53
  "tectonic inclusions," 81
  volcanic greenstone, 56
  See also Great Bar
Ruef, Abe, 123
Rurick (ship), 97

Russian Hill, 34, 154, 199
  agave on, 112
  scrub oaks on, 98

Sacramento-San Joaquin river, 40
Saint Francis Wood, 88
Saint Ignatius Church, 237
San Andreas Fault, 20, 27, 28, 92
San Bruno Mountain range, 32, 61, 207, 222, 223
Sand Dollar Beach, 81
San Francisco, University of, 47
San Francisco Bar. *See* Great Bar
San Francisco City College, 28
  City College Fault, 28, 29
San Francisco Hospital, 46
San Francisco State College, 164
San Mateo County, 35
Scarecrow of Oz, The (Baum), 139
Schlocker, Julius, 28–29, 46
Sea Cliff, 36
Seacliff district, 71
Sea life
  barnacles, 176, 177, 245
  crabs, sand, 185
  Dungeness crabs, 178
  jellyfish, 245
  leopard sharks, 178
  limpets, 177, 245, 246
  mussels, 176, 245
  sand crabs, 185
  sea lions, 153, 192
  seals, 153
  sharks, leopard, 178
  snails, 177
Seal Rocks, 43, 75, 140, 153, 188, 190, 192

Sharon, William, 127
"Sharon" Cottage (Golden Gate Park), 127
Sousa, John Philip, 130
Speedway Meadow (Golden Gate Park), 128, 141, 161
Spreckels, Adolph, 128
Spreckels Lake, 159
Steller, Georg, 153
Stern Grove, 84
Stevenson, Robert Louis, 94, 99
Stinson Beach, 39
Stow, W. W., 125, 127
Stow Lake (Golden Gate Park), 31, 120, 126, 127, 159, 170
Strawberry Hill, 31, 34, 120, 121
  Sweeney's Observatory on, 126
Strybing Arboretum (Golden Gate Park), 96, 146, 159
Sunset district, 28, 33, 34, 48, 58, 89, 136
  as fog belt, 203
Sunset Height. See Golden Gate Heights
Sutro, Adolph, 30, 84, 88, 95, 104, 126, 133–35, 140
Sutro, Mount, 31, 33, 52, 53, 84, 95, 108, 133–35, 160
  Medical Center in, 98
Sutro Baths, 139
Sutro Forest, 30, 52, 85, 86, 100, 135, 150, 154, 186
  Aldea San Miguel, 135
  eucalyptus trees in, 82
  types of trees in, 135
Sutro Heights, 104, 129
Sweeney's Observatory (Strawberry Hill), 126

Tamalpais, Mount, 38, 67, 197, 200, 207
  laurels in, 98
Tank Hill, 31, 53
Telegraph Hill, 27, 30, 32, 78, 115, 160, 194, 199, 203
  acacias on, 108
Tertiary Valley. See Quarry Lake area
Trees
  acacias, 89–93, 108, 122, 135
    Acacia baileyana, 90
    Acacia decurrens, 90
    Acacia longifolia, 90, 148
    Acacia melanoxylon, 90
    Bailey, 90
    black, 90
    silver wattle, 90
    Sydney golden wattle, 90
  ashes, 135
  aspens, 82
  Atlas cedar, 129
  Australian tea tree, 148
  Bailey acacia, 90
  bay, 98
  beeches, 135
  black acacia, 90
  blue gum eucalyptus, 87, 88, 100, 102, 103, 113, 135
  buckeyes, 98
  cedar, Atlas, 129
  cottonwoods, 82
  cypress, 52, 53, 84, 91, 93–96, 135, 136, 149, 226
    Monterey, 84, 91, 93–96, 104, 105, 113, 122, 141, 150, 223
  Douglas fir, 25, 207
  elms, 116, 201
  eucalyptus, 52, 72, 73, 82, 122, 199, 226
    blue gum, 87, 88, 100, 102, 103, 113, 135

  covered pods on, 103
  Eucalyptus cinerea, 88–89
  Eucalyptus ficifolia, 87–88
  Eucalyptus globulus, 87
  Eucalpytus polyanthemos, 88
  Eucalyptus pulverulenta, 88
  eucalyptus rush, 84–86
  Eucalyptus viminalis, 87
  first large plantings of, 83
  gum, 87–88
  major planters of, 83–84
  manna gum, 87, 88, 101
  ribbon gum, 87
  silver-dollar, 88, 102
  "skyscraper," 87
  varieties of, 86–89
  fir, Douglas, 25, 207
  gum, 87–88
  laurels, 98
    bay trees, 98
    Umbellularia californica, 98
  Leptospermum, 148
  live oak, 25, 98, 99, 117, 148, 207
  Lombardy poplars, 82
  manna gum eucalyptus, 87, 88, 101
  maples, 135
  Monterey cypress, 84, 91, 93–96, 104, 105, 113, 122, 141, 150, 223
  Monterey pines, 31, 54, 71, 84, 91–93, 106, 122, 135, 150
  Norfolk Island pines, 116, 117

oaks
    live, 25, 98, 99, 117,
        148, 207
    Quercus agrifolia, 98
    scrub, 98
pines, 31, 54, 71, 82, 84,
    91–93, 95, 104,
    135, 226
    history of in Califor-
        nia, 91–92
    Monterey, 31, 54, 71,
        84, 91–93, 106,
        122, 135, 150
    Norfolk Island, 116,
        117
poplars, Lombardy, 82
raintrees, 89–93
redwoods, 25, 98
ribbon gum eucalyptus,
    87
scrub oak, 98
Sequoia gigantea, 116
silver-dollar eucalyptus,
    88, 102
silver wattle acacia, 90
"skyscraper" eucalyptus,
    87
sycamores, 116, 117, 261
Sydney golden wattle
    acacia, 90
tea tree, Australian, 148
Twin Peaks, 27, 30, 31,
    32, 33, 48, 49, 50,
    116, 120, 137, 156,
    160, 191, 194, 197,
    207, 208, 210, 211

Union Square, 87, 202
United States Geological
    Survey, 28

Vallejo, Mariano Guada-
    lupe, 134
Vancouver, George, 97
Van Gogh, Vincent, 159
Visitacion Valley, 28
Vista Point, 194

Washerwoman's Lagoon,
    49
Weather. *See under* Cli-
    mate
West Speedway Meadow
    (Golden Gate
    Park), 128, 141
Wildlife
    alligators, 186
    bears, grizzly, 150
    birds. *See* main entry
    brush rabbits, 151
    burrowing mice, 151
    butterflies, Monarch,
        187
    California ground squir-
        rels, 181
    California sea lions, 153
    cottontail rabbits, 151
    coyotes, 151
    deer, 150
    Eastern gray squirrels,
        150, 181
    elk, 150
    foxes, 151, 152
        gray, 151, 186
    gophers, 151
    gray squirrels, Eastern,
        150, 181
    grizzly bears, 150
    ground squirrels, Califor-
        nia, 181
    iguanas, 186

jack rabbits, 151
kinkajous, 186
Mephitis mephitis, 152
mice, burrowing, 151
moles, 151
Monarch   butterflies,
    187
otters, 150
possums, 150, 151, 152
rabbits, 151
    brush, 151
    cottontail, 151
    jack, 151
raccoons, 150, 151, 152,
    154, 186
sea lions, 153
    California, 153
    Steller, 153, 192
seals, 153
skunks
    spotted, 152
    striped, 152
squirrels
    California   ground,
        181
    Eastern   gray,   150,
        181
    Steller sea lions, 153,
        192
    striped skunks, 152
    weasels, 151, 152
    wildcats, 151
Willis, Bailey, 47
Winds. *See under* Climate
Woodward's Gardens, re-
    placement of, 122
Wright, Frank Lloyd, 83

Young, Mike H. de, 130–
    31

GOLDEN GATE PARK

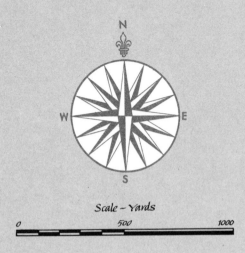

Scale – Yards

0   500   1000

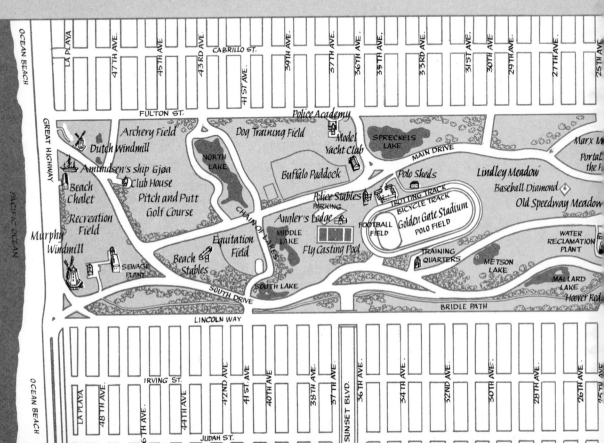